Women, Gender, AND
Christian Community

Women, Gender,
and
Christian Community

Jane Dempsey Douglass
James F. Kay
editors

Westminster John Knox Press
Louisville, Kentucky

Scripture quotations from the New Revised Standard Version
of the Bible are copyright © 1989 by the Division of Christian Education
of the National Council of the Churches of Christ in the U.S.A.
and are used by permission.

Book design by Jennifer K. Cox
Cover design by Ken Herndon
Cover illustrations: (Left) Rembrandt Harmensz. van Rijn.
Portrait of Hendrickje Stoffels. *Louvre, Paris, France.*
(Right): Rembrandt Harmensz. van Rijn. Portrait of a Man.
Kunsthistorisches Museum, Vienna, Austria.

First edition
Published by Westminster John Knox Press
Louisville, Kentucky

This book is printed on acid-free paper that meets the
American National Standards Institute Z39.48 standard. ∞

PRINTED IN THE UNITED STATES OF AMERICA
97 98 99 00 01 02 03 04 05 06 — 10 9 8 7 6 5 4 3 2 1

Library of Congress Cataloging-in-Publication Data

Women, gender, and Christian community / Jane Dempsey Douglass
and James F. Kay, editors. — 1st ed.
    p.   cm.
Includes bibliographical references.
ISBN 0-664-25728-3 (alk. paper)
    1. Feminist theology. I. Douglass, E. Jane Dempsey.   II. Kay,
James F., date.
BT83.55.W64   1997
230'.082—dc21
                                                        96-40009

To Freda A. Gardner,
first woman professor at Princeton Theological Seminary
and untiring advocate for partnership of women and men
in the church.

Contents

Part II. Gender Issues
in the Life of the Christian Community

Preface

Women and men in Christian communities have not found it easy to talk about gender issues together. We discovered recently in the firestorm over the "Re-imagining Conference" just how explosive these issues still are when they are related to religion, even in mainstream churches in North America. Precisely for that reason, conversation about gender issues, especially as they relate to faith, must be fostered in theological seminaries and in congregations where people of goodwill can learn to hear one another with open hearts and open minds.

This book is intended to encourage conversation between women and men about some of the gender issues that women have been pressing for some time. Does the Bible truly speak good news to women? If God is spirit and neither male nor female, why has the church insisted on referring to God with male pronouns and male images? Does not the Bible itself use female images for God? Can a spirituality developed by men out of their experience nourish the lives of women? How can men and women work together in churches with dignity, communicate clearly with one another, make decisions together as full partners? How can it be that, even in the church, women still risk sexual exploitation? How can Christians who truly respect the scriptures and churchly tradition justify the ordination of women as ministers, elders, and deacons?

The chapters in this book have been written by members of the Princeton Theological Seminary faculty—Christian men and women, ministers, elders, and lay people. These chapters grow out of ongoing teaching and research, the substance of regular faculty work. Twenty years ago gender questions tended to be regarded simply as women's questions. Today in mainstream American theological seminaries, faculty men, too, increasingly understand these questions to be of concern to the whole community; they are questions for which the whole community has responsibility. Faculty members, both male and female, are learning to deal with the gender issues that arise from the material with which they work, to recognize the distinctive ways in which women and men bring their different life experiences to their reading of texts, their social interaction, their theological construction and analysis, and their preaching.

The genesis of this book was conversation among the faculty members about how they might share with the wider church community their research and thinking about gender issues, thereby opening a broader conversation. Last year Professor Choon-Leong Seow invited all members of the faculty to offer chapters for a book on "Gender, Sexuality, and Theological Imagination." The outpouring of suggestions led him to restrict his book to the single topic, *Homosexuality and Christian Community* (Louisville, Ky.: Westminster John Knox Press, 1996), a topic that was then under intensive study in the Presbyterian Church (U.S.A.). Soon after the book appeared in print, faculty members at their weekly luncheons asked one another when a book on gender issues could be produced, because the need for conversation in the churches remains urgent. The whole faculty was again invited to propose chapters for such a book, and again the faculty's support for the project proved enthusiastic.

The topics discussed here fall into two parts. Part 1 is titled "Reading Scripture Through the Lens of Gender Issues." We will see that recent discussion of gender issues in scripture stands in a long tradition going back to the beginnings of the church.

Patrick D. Miller, in chapter 1, explores the role of imagination in the work of the biblical interpreter, reflecting especially on imagining God in relation to gender issues. In chapter 2, Katharine Doob Sakenfeld takes up particularly difficult texts in the Hebrew scriptures that deal with women—the stories of Deborah and Jael—and dialogues with Asian women about them. Choon-Leong Seow (chapter 3) analyzes another text, Ecclesiastes 7:26–29, which has long been used against women, and brings a fresh perspective on its significance for wisdom and folly. Kathleen E. McVey (chapter 4) focuses on Sophia (Wisdom) and other female imagery for the divine in the theology of Clement of Alexandria, showing how skillfully this third-century thinker uses such biblical imagery. In chapter 5, Paul Rorem offers a variety of examples of male and female imagery for God and the soul in the theological writings of medieval men and women, especially the mystics. Jane Dempsey Douglass (chapter 6) observes that some women writing about the Bible during the Reformation period focus on different texts from those emphasized by the male theologians of the period; the women take up texts that offer freedom from male domination, portray women as acting boldly, and are understood to call women and men to equal responsibility.

Part 2 is titled "Gender Issues in the Life of the Christian Community." In chapter 7, Nancy J. Duff explores how the teaching of vocation addresses issues of gender as they relate to motherhood and relations between men and women in marriage. Next, David Willis (chapter 8) lays out a theological argument that the catholicity of the church requires the freedom to ordain women. James F. Kay, in chapter 9, analyzes the crucial role of baptism for the equality of women and men in the church and evaluates the language of recent baptismal liturgies as to their effectiveness in proclaiming this teaching for the church. In chapter 10, Leonora Tubbs Tisdale identifies some styles of language used by women in preaching that are different from those of men and evaluates the effectiveness of those

Preface

styles for all preachers. Janet L. Weathers (chapter 11) is concerned with understanding patterns of communication between women and men in small groups within the church and indicates ways to make it more effective. Donald Capps (chapter 12) takes up the problem of sexual misconduct by male pastors with female parishioners, arguing for acknowledging the factor of desire in seeking ways to avoid pastoral abuses of power. Carol Lakey Hess (chapter 13) evaluates the usefulness for women's lives of classical spiritual disciplines with their emphasis on humility and obedience, taking into account their impact on women's self-esteem.

The authors reflect differing approaches to theology and to gender questions. Nonetheless, we share a commitment to a vision of the church where women as well as men can be full participants. The range of our voices is not as wide as one might like to hear. Missing, for example, are *mujerista* and womanist voices, so important to the American church scene. These chapters simply represent a sampling of the work being done here at Princeton Theological Seminary. This work has been encouraged at the Seminary for twenty-five years by the Women's Center, which is celebrating its anniversary this year with a series of forums for the whole campus community on the themes of this book.

Our concerns for the full partnership of women and men extend far beyond our local context, however. We are mindful that the program of the Ecumenical Decade of Churches in Solidarity with Women (1988–98) is challenging all churches around the world to support women's struggle for an equal place in the church and society, to affirm women's contributions to the church's life across the ages, and to open themselves to the gifts and special perspectives of women for the mission of the church and a more just society. We have in mind also the PACT program of the World Alliance of Reformed Churches in support of the goals of the Ecumenical Decade: the program to affirm, challenge, and transform so that women and men may be full partners in God's mission in church and society. In support of such efforts, therefore, we offer these chapters as an expression of solidarity with women around the world.

The editors are grateful that our colleagues care so deeply about the importance of gender issues in the church today and that they were willing to lay aside other pressing tasks to engage in this conversation with the church. We also express our appreciation to Steven R. Bechtler of *The Princeton Seminary Bulletin* for his editorial assistance and to our editor Stephanie Egnotovich of Westminster John Knox Press for her encouragement of this project.

Jane Dempsey Douglass
James F. Kay

Contributors

Donald Capps, William Harte Felmeth Professor of Pastoral Theology, Princeton Theological Seminary, Princeton, New Jersey

Jane Dempsey Douglass, Hazel Thompson McCord Professor of Historical Theology, Princeton Theological Seminary, Princeton, New Jersey

Nancy J. Duff, Associate Professor of Theological Ethics, Princeton Theological Seminary, Princeton, New Jersey

Carol Lakey Hess, Assistant Professor of Christian Education, Princeton Theological Seminary, Princeton, New Jersey

James F. Kay, Associate Professor of Homiletics and Liturgics, Princeton Theological Seminary, Princeton, New Jersey

Kathleen E. McVey, Joseph Ross Stevenson Professor of Church History, Princeton Theological Seminary, Princeton, New Jersey

Patrick D. Miller, Charles T. Haley Professor of Old Testament Theology, Princeton Theological Seminary, Princeton, New Jersey

Paul Rorem, Benjamin B. Warfield Associate Professor of Medieval Church History, Princeton Theological Seminary, Princeton, New Jersey

Katharine Doob Sakenfeld, William Albright Eisenberger Professor of Old Testament Literature and Exegesis, and Director of Ph.D. Studies, Princeton Theological Seminary, Princeton, New Jersey

Choon-Leong Seow, Henry Snyder Gehman Professor of Old Testament Language and Literature, Princeton Theological Seminary, Princeton, New Jersey

Leonora Tubbs Tisdale, Associate Professor of Preaching and Worship, Princeton Theological Seminary, Princeton, New Jersey

Janet L. Weathers, Assistant Professor of Speech Communication in Ministry, Princeton Theological Seminary, Princeton, New Jersey

David Willis, Charles Hodge Professor of Systematic Theology, Princeton Theological Seminary, Princeton, New Jersey

Part I

Reading Scripture
Through the Lens of Gender Issues

1

Imagining God

In contemporary discussion about the role of the feminine in the life and language of faith, the sharpest debates continue to center around the relation of gender to our notions of God. In the early 1970s, the committee preparing a revision of the Revised Standard Version of the Bible—the present NRSV—accepted without hesitation the mandate from its parent body, the National Council of Churches, to provide a translation that would be inclusive in its language with reference to gender; but it also decided, more cautiously, that inclusiveness would be carried out only with regard to language about human beings but not for language about God. When another committee, working also under the aegis of the National Council of Churches, produced *An Inclusive Language Lectionary,* it created an uproar and vigorous attacks in the media as well as in theological circles, to no small degree because of its commitment to translating in ways that would eliminate gender identifications or restrictions in reference to either God or Jesus. While there was no attempt to deny the masculinity of Jesus, terminology that seemed to focus on that, or could be understood as doing so, was changed. Thus the christological title customarily translated into English as "Son of Man" was translated as "the Human One," and the title "Son of God" was translated as "Child of God." These translations are perfectly defensible both linguistically and theologically. Long before there was any focus at all on gender issues, theologians had been clear that the incarnation had to do with the *humanity* of Jesus and was not to be understood as gender referential in a substantive way. But once an explicit effort to clarify that point was underway, in relation to changing language practices, reaction burst forth in vigorous fashion and has not abated. There are many who are very careful about eliminating gender references in their language about human beings, unless gender distinction is intended, but continue to use masculine, and only masculine, language with reference to God and Jesus. In the context of contemporary English usage moving toward the elimination of "man" language as a way of speaking about human beings in general, the continued use of masculine language in speaking about God serves now only to heighten or claim a gender reference in deity that was not intended as much before, even if it ended up making such reference implicitly.

What is evident in the very different reactions to changing language about human beings and changing it about God, even when the change could be argued to be a conservative one to avoid developing gender-specific notions of God, is the sensitivity of the theological and public minds with regard to anything that has to do with God and the ways we think about, speak of, and worship God. It is not surprising, therefore, that the church, or at least those denominations involved, was greatly stirred up over the Re-imagining Conference in 1993, which gathered together primarily women from various denominations all over the world to talk and think about imagining God in different ways and to engage in worship that reflected such "re-imaging," specifically with regard to feminine dimensions in our understanding of deity.

While the ultimate aim of this chapter is to argue *for* the activity of imagination and the attention to gender in the theological enterprise, it should be acknowledged at the start that there is something important in the questions raised about these matters. One of the clearest motifs of scripture is the prophetic critique against any worship that is incompatible with the First and Second Commandments, prohibiting the worship of any other God but the Lord of Israel and the worship of any image of that God or of any other god. For those who live in the context of the biblical tradition, the conformity of Christian worship and faith to the First Commandment is no small matter. It defines who we are and what we are about in this world. It is not subject to malleability or to occasional departures. If the Lord of Israel is the one who made us and the world of which we are a part, if the Lord of Israel is the only one who can take away our fear and save us in our trouble, if the Lord of Israel has alone brought us to this place and is alone our hope for the future, then all our trust and all our adoration are placed there and nowhere else. That happens to be a piece of good news serving to make relative all the other demands and claims on our life.

But if all that is indeed true, it is a reality we cannot enter and leave, looking for some other cosmic system, some other ground to stand on, some other deliverer. For one thing, there isn't any; furthermore, our very identity is established by the exclusive worship of this God who has loved us and redeemed us. We cannot walk two ways at the same time. We cannot live in two different worlds at the same time. The God who speaks to us in scripture is not friendly toward other gods or tolerant of divided loyalties. The biblical stories of the Lord's war against the other gods (for example, the conflict with Baal at Mt. Carmel in 1 Kings 18; cf. Psalm 82) is a narrative way of telling us that there are all sorts of possibilities out there to tempt our worship and allegiance, but the maker of heaven and earth is a jealous God and will have none of it.

One of the chief ways in which we attempt to domesticate God is by assuming a kind of friendliness, selflessness, and tolerance on the part of God that we hope is present in all of us. We are all too inclined in our worship to confirm Feuerbach's challenge and to worship a God who is made in our own image. The jealousy and wrath of God are reminders that God is meant not to be likable but to be God. The joy and praise we render are to the God who has redeemed us and taken away our fears so that we can live in this world; the celebration is over the fact that the power that undergirds everything is clearly loving and on our side. But the cross tells us that it is a painful love, and the First Commandment tells us it cannot be played with or taken for granted.

When people begin to talk about re-imagining God, therefore, reaction is not unexpected, especially in light of the common assumption that the imagination is a sphere of the mind to be contrasted with reality. It sounds as if revelation is being ignored and one is simply constructing the notion of God willy-nilly, however one pleases, and without reference to scripture and the tradition that grows out of scripture. Imagining God seems to be another way of choosing other gods to worship, that is, gods who fit our desires and preferences.

In other contexts, however, serious attention is being given in these times to the realm of the *imagination* as a central locus of *revelation*[1] as well as the ground of *preaching and proclamation*.[2] Indeed, it is rather ironic that the Re-imagining Conference has created such a furor precisely at the time that theology—perhaps in a postmodern mode, though one does not have to assume that context to let the imagination have its theological play—through various voices asserts the significance of the imagination in and for its work.[3] Nor can one identify this focus on the role of imagination in theology as essentially a liberal or radical enterprise that departs from tradition and scripture, particularly in the contemporary context of theology. In the work of Gordon Kaufman, it may be that—or seem to be—though no theologian has worked any harder at serious "construction" of a contemporary doctrine of God.[4] But in Garrett Green, contemporary theology presents an essentially conservative, tradition-oriented theologian—with some sympathy toward feminist concerns but not toward modifying and expanding theological language—reminding us of the revelatory significance of the imagination.[5] While he notes the way in which describing religion as an act of imagination has tended to lead "in a reductionist direction, implying that religion is the product of human needs, the projection of this-worldly subjectivity onto an illusory screen of other-worldly objectivity," he does not think that is inevitable.[6] Rather, he argues that the act of imagining is quite different from "imaging" God, an activity that is in danger of being idolatrous:

> The religious imagination does not "image" God (i.e., construct some kind of picture of God) but *imagines* God (i.e., thinks of God according

to a paradigm). The paradigmatic imagination is not mimetic but analogical; it shows us not what God *is* but what God is *like*. (Idolatry, reduced to an epigram, confuses the "is" with the "as.")[7]

Similarly, Walter Brueggemann lifts up the imagination precisely in relation
to the interpretation of scripture as he notes, with Green, that "the canon
of Scripture provides the paradigm through which the faithful practice
imagination."[8] David Kelsey has argued for the centrality of "imaginative
construals" in the theological task. In his words:

> [A]t the root of a theological position there is an imaginative act in which
> a theologian tries to catch up in a single metaphorical judgment the full
> complexity of God's presence in, through, and over-against the activities
> comprising the church's common life and which, in turn, both provides
> the *discrimen* against which the theology criticizes the church's current
> forms of speech and life, and determines the peculiar "shape" of the "po-
> sition."[9]

The imagination is an indispensable part of our theological work. It is
also a risky and dangerous sphere of operation. The verbal associations between "imagining" and "imaging" are so close that one may easily speak
the one when intending the other. Imagining is an act of imaging.[10] From
the scriptures we learn that imaging God is both necessary and idolatrous.
We live, theologically, between imagining in a way that makes fear and
worship and obedience possible, that provides the grounds of hope and
trust without which human existence is hardly possible, and imaging in a
way that turns God and the matters of faith into utensils of human ambition, power, and self-interest. To pray to the Father, to look to the Rock,
to be led by the Shepherd, to bow before the Ruler—all of these are acts
of Christian, indeed, of religious existence that belong to the very nature
of faith in God. Such images give concreteness to that which is not concrete. They let us picture what cannot be pictured, enable us to connect
with a source we cannot touch, see, feel, or locate.

Without such imagining, faith in a God who is personal, involved with
human life and this world, would be most difficult. Nor is such imagining
an arbitrary act. What human life needs joins with what human life is
given—in scripture. The reliance on scripture that has been an integral part
of the life of many Christians and Jews is not simply out of some sense of
duty or religious requirement but because there one finds the story and the
images that make sense of our existence and ground it in a transcendent
Other who claims our lives and makes them good and true—or lets us know
when they are not. The imagination is at work in the formation of scripture and in its reception.

In more traditional terms, we speak of that as the work of the Spirit, although neither imagination nor Spirit is identical with the other or exhausted by the other. It is no accident that where fresh winds of faith and

powerful acts of imagination have burst forth in the life of the church—from Pentecost to the Reformation to a Re-imagining Conference—some people have seen the Spirit at work, whereas others have seen confusion and idolatry. The Spirit blows where it will, and our imagining may be the construction of idols. No one is more perilously and constantly on the edge of breaking the commandment against idolatry than the theologian, the one who thinks and speaks about God. The image may become the idol.

In our time, we have discovered, in the imagery of God the Father, how close we have come to turning the revelatory imagination into a factory for idols. Every time we begin the Lord's Prayer, we direct our minds and hearts toward one who cares in whose "hands"—so the imaging of the imagination suggests—we place our lives. Yet each time we do that, we also risk making the God who has created us plastic and concrete; we risk claiming to know too much, letting the metaphor so become the reality that it becomes an idol. Indeed, the equation of the metaphor, the image, with reality is where idolatry happens. The evoking of metaphors as an act of imagination whose relation to reality is elusive, yes and no, is what theological work is all about. Surely some images are more yes and some more no, but there are none that are unambiguously yes and few that are unambiguously no. Whenever we take up images of God, we are, as Deuteronomy 4 reminds us, playing with fire. They may illumine and represent God, or—as fire often does—they may consume us. Either way, it is a dangerous business.

What then about re-imagining? Is that part of the theological enterprise, or is it merely the perversion of the authentic and faithful imagining that arises out of the scriptural paradigm? I recall the joke that went around a couple of decades ago about the reporter who got an interview with God and, when pressed afterward to tell the world what God looked like, responded, "She's black." Most of us laughed, but some among us said, "That's my God." Or one remembers the sensational sculpture "Christa" that was pictured on the front pages of newspapers across the country several years ago, a crucifix on which hung a Christ with breasts. Scandalous, said most of us. But others said, "That's my Jesus."

In our time, we often decry the absence of theological giants, the Barths and the Bultmanns who shake the theological fortresses we have built and force us into new thinking. Meanwhile, just such shaking of the foundations has been going on around us, but it is less in singular, deep theological voices and more in a groundswell of witnesses whose re-imagining of God in different colors and images points us afresh to the reality that is God, indeed the God who made us and speaks to us constantly through scripture, whose blackness and breasts may be the most powerful revelatory imagining of the incarnation, of the word made flesh, that our minds—at least in this moment—can receive. So also the evocation of sophia/wisdom, an image of God that is—like all our images—both yes and no and—like all the images that sustain us in any authentic way—rooted deeply in scripture, should provide an impetus for theological work more than for ecclesiastical resolutions.

It may also suggest the need for more imaginative elbowroom in our contemporary theology, more willingness to ask for the connections between Christian tradition and, for example, a feminist's invoking of female figures from other faiths or lifting up a minor element of biblical tradition into major focus, and more hesitancy at drawing sharp lines, particularly by male theologians, whose guardianship of the faith through the ages has sometimes been a barrier to the authentic vision of God. The largely—though not totally—negative male reaction to primarily female acts of re-imagination is something we ought to ponder. It is at least consistent with a common tendency of the community of faith—from biblical times to the present—to judge a particularly feminine perspective or religious activity as heterodox.

In the Bible, that tendency is seen especially in the way in which women are particularly, though not exclusively, associated with activities around goddess worship or around the *asherah*. The *asherah* was either the consort of Yahweh the God of Israel or, more likely, a cult object associated with the worship of Yahweh but one that was feminine in linguistic form, and possibly in its imagery, and could be separated from the deity and treated independently, thus becoming in effect an idol. There is inscriptional evidence from ancient Israel suggesting that veneration of "Yahweh and his *asherah*" was carried out by persons, including males, who saw themselves as good and faithful worshipers of the God of Israel and not idolators.

The significance of the involvement of women in such activities is not altogether clear. It may have been that women were generally marginalized in most of the formal cultic activities of orthodox and public religion and so forced into marginally acceptable to unacceptable roles from that perspective.[11] One notices also, however, that the women's cultic activities were of the sort that women customarily carried out in society and domestic life generally, for example, weaving and cooking.[12] In both instances, the usually domestic activities were explicitly cultic. The domestic role of women is attested in these practices, but it is brought into the cultic. That suggests that the cult of the goddess or the cult of the *asherah,* whether as a hypostatized dimension of the Lord of Israel or as a goddess, was particularly open to the participation of women and in a way that incorporated their customary activities as women into its ritual and cultic life. Place was made for women and for women's activities and concerns in these aberrant practices in a way that seems to have been much less the case in the more normative or official forms of Israelite religion. Phyllis Bird concludes: "Peculiarly or predominantly female forms of ritual and worship are suggested in the canonical sources *only* in reference to heterodox cults."[13]

Sophia/Wisdom seems new and strange to us—though scripture tells us she was there at the creation (Prov. 8:22–31). We are familiar with a Logos Christology that is rooted in the Gospel of John, and especially John 1, which speaks of the Logos/Word being in the beginning with God and being God. We are less familiar with a Sophia Christology, but the two are not far apart.[14] Commentaries on Proverbs 8 and on John 1 that pay attention to intertestamental connections regularly associate these texts with each other. The fact that one, Sophia/Wisdom, seems to have her roots primarily in the Old Testament places her more on the margin of our theological and christological discussion than the other, Logos/Word, which is explicitly associated with Jesus Christ in the New Testament. But the New Testament also makes a clear identification between Christ and Sophia in 1 Corinthians:

> But we proclaim Christ crucified, a stumbling block to Jews and foolishness to Gentiles, but to those who are the called, both Jews and Greeks, Christ the power of God and the wisdom (*sophia*) of God. (1:23–24)

> He is the source of your life in Christ Jesus, who became for us wisdom (*sophia*) from God. (1:30)

The feminine character of Sophia/Wisdom seems to press her even further outside the camp. But that depends very much on who defines the circle of faith and the hermeneutical and theological rules they use to do that. In the Eastern tradition of the church, the identification of Christ with Wisdom maintained a strong presence. The very strong reaction to the veneration of Wisdom may be one more sign of the provincialism of many of us in Western Christianity.

The critical issue raised, therefore, by the Re-imagining Conference may be finally not whether its theology and worship failed to conform to the First Commandment but who it is that defines that conformity. The line between heterodoxy and orthodoxy depends to some degree upon who is drawing it. The marginality of women in the liturgy of the Christian community and in its theological formulations continues. The definitions of conformity and the condemnations of what does not conform are made largely by a male-oriented theological and political structure.[15] Such a structure is not inherently wrong, but it is inevitably restricted in its perspective on faith and reality.

If one can speak of "the circle of faith," as I think one can, it is truly a circle and not a box. The lines of circumference are always fuzzy and imprecise, so that one may not always know how close one is to being "in" or "out."[16] Scripture itself reminds us that some voices dwell on the outskirts of faith's camp, so much so that sometimes they seem to be, indeed, outside the camp. One thinks of Ecclesiastes in this regard, but Martin Luther would have argued the case against other biblical voices also. Yet Christian faith claims God's revelation in the skeptical faith of Ecclesiastes, even if its themes seem like a radical rejection of the Mosaic faith. The Preacher's problem was less the too-much-faith of syncretism than the too-little-faith of nihilism. The latter may be no less a danger to the proper worship of God than the former. Still, Ecclesiastes remains inside the circle, inside the camp.

The process of imagining and re-imagining is always subject to critique. That is how theology develops. It is always grounded in scripture. That is what keeps it Christian. If those two things are happening—scriptural rootage and openness to criticism—then a theological re-imagination that is particularly open to the feminine may be a significant step of faithfulness and toward the truth about the God who is revealed in Jesus Christ.

Notes

This chapter is an expansion and development of thoughts first set forth in an editorial with the same title in *Theology Today* 51 (1994): 341–44.

1. See, for example, Garrett Green, *Imagining God* (San Francisco: Harper & Row, 1989). Green discusses in his first chapter some of the history of the place of imagination in religious thinking.
2. See, for example, Walter Brueggemann, *Texts Under Negotiation: The Bible and the Postmodern Imagination* (Minneapolis: Fortress Press, 1993).
3. In addition to the works cited in nn. 1 and 2, see David Kelsey, *The Uses of Scripture in Recent Theology* (Philadelphia: Fortress Press, 1975); David Tracy, *The Analogical Imagination: Christian Theology and the Culture of Pluralism* (New York: Crossroad, 1981); David Bryant, *Faith and the Play of Imagination: On the Role of Imagination in Religion* (Macon, Ga.: Mercer University Press, 1989); Maria Harris, *Teaching and Religious Imagination* (San Francisco: Harper & Row, 1987). In his first chapter, Brueggemann has some brief but helpful discussion of some of these works, their relation to each other, and their contribution to what he understands by postmodern interpretation.
4. See Gordon Kaufman's *An Essay on Theological Method,* rev. ed. (Atlanta: Scholars Press, 1995) and *The Theological Imagination: Constructing the Concept of God* (Philadelphia: Westminster Press, 1981). In a response to Kaufman's approach, Ronald Thiemann has argued against setting revelation and imagination in opposition to each other ("Revelation and Imaginative Construction," *Journal of Religion* 61 [1981]: 242–63; see his discussion of both Kelsey and Kaufman in *Revelation and Theology: The Gospel as Narrated Promise* [Notre Dame, Ind.: University of Notre Dame Press, 1985], 47–70).
5. Green has been specifically critical of the move toward inclusive and feminine language for God. See, for example, *Imagining God,* 164 n. 18, and

his essay "The Gender of God and the Theology of Metaphor," in *Speaking the Christian God: The Holy Trinity and the Challenge of Feminism*, ed. Alvin F. Kimel, Jr. (Grand Rapids: Wm. B. Eerdmans, 1992).

6. Green, *Imagining God,* 26.
7. Ibid., 93.
8. Brueggemann, *Texts Under Negotiation,* 14; citing Green's chap. 6, "The Normative Vision: The Function of Scripture."
9. Kelsey, *The Uses of Scripture in Recent Theology,* 163.
10. But note in this regard Green's caution indicated above about equating image and imagination. His call for understanding imagination as the taking of *paradigms* to explore the patterns of the larger world is quite important to the discussion about God and the place of the feminine in the theological construction. So also is his insistence on the *open-endedness* of all such terms and notions as "paradigm," "model," "metaphor," and "myth," which are the analogical vehicles for the religious imagination (See Green, *Imagining God,* 69–70).
11. See Phyllis Bird, "The Place of Women in the Israelite Cultus," in *Ancient Israelite Religion* (Philadelphia: Fortress Press, 1987), 397–419.
12. See the weaving of "houses" or "coverings" for the *asherah* in 2 Kings 23:7 and the cooking of cakes for the Queen of Heaven in Jeremiah 7:18 and 44:19.
13. Bird, "The Place of Women," 409 (italics mine). Bird goes on to suggest: "Of possible greater significance for an understanding of women's religious participation and the total religious life of the community is the hidden realm of women's rituals and devotions that take place entirely within the domestic sphere and/or in the company of other women. Cross-cultural studies show that these often constitute the emotional center of women's religious life as well as the bulk of their religious activity, especially where their participation in the central cultus is limited. For such practices, however, we have little or no direct testimony, as this order of religious practice is generally seen as unworthy of note unless it challenges or undermines the central cultus. (Women's rites may even be unknown to men, who have no part in them.) . . . The line between religion and magic or orthodox and heterodox is more difficult to draw in this realm of practice and belief since the controls of the central cultus, its priesthood and theology, are largely absent. Like folk religion everywhere, it is typically seen as debased or corrupted and often as syncretistic" (409–10).
14. For more extensive discussion of the biblical and theological grounding for Sophia as a christological and theological image, see Elisabeth Schüssler Fiorenza, *In Memory of Her: A Feminist Theological Reconstruction of Christian Origins* (New York: Crossroad, 1984), 130–40; and Elizabeth Johnson, *She Who Is: The Mystery of God in Feminist Theological Discourse* (New York: Crossroad, 1993).
15. Then as now, of course, women were also a part of, and expressed the more normative forms of, religious life and theological formulation. The issue is whether the experience of women in general, to the extent that it differs from that of men, is a part of, and contributes to the imaginative

receptivity of, revelation or whether that experience ends up seeming strange and thus aberrant because it is not the experience of the dominant, that is, male, group.

16. Here is the rationale for the former Presbyterian custom, little practiced, I think, of having ordained ministers and elders inform their presbytery of any matter of theology on which they thought they might have departed from the "system of doctrine" to which they had subscribed in their ordination vows. It was the duty of the larger group, not the individual by himself or herself, to make decisions about whether the present belief was in fact a departure, that is, a movement fully outside the circle of faith as defined in the confessional tradition. Actual practice revealed the circle to be quite malleable, with plenty of room to move around its edges.

2

Deborah, Jael, and Sisera's Mother: Reading the Scriptures in Cross-Cultural Context

In recent years biblical scholarship has been moving rapidly toward the recognition that the gender and culture of biblical interpreters inevitably affect their interpretations of the text and even the questions they think to put to the text. Given this reality, one of the primary ways to develop fresh questions and fresh understandings is to engage in self-conscious listening to the work of persons different in background from oneself. While a process of testing and correcting had long gone on within the traditional "guild" of primarily male, North Atlantic biblical scholars, North Atlantic women's voices have been added to the mix in significant numbers only in the last decade, and voices of women and men from Asia, Africa, and Latin America still remain on the margins of the North Atlantic conversation. As a North American white feminist, I have sought to make a beginning of breaking through this barrier for myself by visiting in Asia and participating in Bible studies led by Asian Christian women, both lay and theologically trained. This chapter, originally presented as part of the Brueggemann Lectureship at Eden Seminary in 1996, suggests some ways in which those conversations have given a new complexity and freshness to my understanding of Judges 4—5.

Although any picture of women in public leadership still bothers some contemporary Christians, the story of Deborah and Jael is challenging to many others because the public leadership roles of these two women involve military action. In my experience, these chapters are uncomfortable reading for both women and men in white middle/upper-class North America. I do not think I have ever heard a sermon on these chapters. I did not learn these stories in Sunday school (though I did learn about Samson and about David and Goliath). I know that even as a woman with a special interest in biblical stories about women I have, as I look back on my work, carefully avoided studying these texts.

Yet my experiences with women in Asia have challenged me to take a closer look at these stories. Women whom I met in the Philippines and in Korea in particular were very fond of these stories. Filipino women told me of songs being sung in rural areas that celebrate the heroic deeds of women who, by guerrilla warfare, have challenged oppressive government policies. As the situation remains politically unstable, these songs are still sung in secret, unrecorded, not written down. The women with whom I spoke knew of such songs only by hearsay; they had not themselves participated in the events or sat with the singers. Nonetheless, they wanted to express support in some way for these women who had used force to challenge what they perceived as a military dictatorship.

So also in Korea, stories are told of women who have brought to ruin enemy forces by killing a leader of an invading or occupying military power. Some are classic stories relating to earlier periods of Korean history, but others are relatively contemporary, relating to the Japanese occupation of Korea during the first half of the twentieth century.

Encountering such positive attitudes, even enthusiasm, for Bible chapters that I and my North American friends have personally found uncomfortable has called me to reconsider my own view, as well as to ask on what grounds I might want to query the view of my Asian friends. Listening across cultural and national boundaries has provided an opportunity for growing in faith and in deeper understanding of scripture.

A brief overview of the text will set the stage. As Judges 4 opens, we learn that because of the Israelites' wrongdoing they have been living under the heel of Canaanite oppression for twenty years. Two leaders of these Canaanites are introduced: King Jabin (who has no real narrative role in the story) and Sisera, his general, or army commander.

The Israelites cry out to God from their distress, a motif familiar from the opening of the story of the exodus from Egypt, as well as from the earlier chapters of Judges. Often when the Israelites cry out to God the text reports immediately that God heard their cry and undertook a response. In the two previous examples in Judges (3:9, 15) we are told at once that God raised up a deliverer, and the deliverer's name is given. But here the divine response is reported less directly. The narrator does turn immediately to introduce an Israelite leader, Deborah, but it is not self-evident that she is to be the deliverer; indeed, the identity of the deliverer is made obscure to heighten the narrative tension.

We learn that Deborah was a "prophet" and that she "was judging Israel" (v. 4). In one short verse she is introduced as participating in two of Israel's most important leadership roles. In the book of Judges, the function of the judging role seems to be twofold: Judges were sometimes those to whom cases or disputes could be brought for decision; in other instances they were charismatic leaders raised up by God, usually for a military emergency. Deborah is presented to us in both of these judging functions. In 4:5 Deborah is introduced as one who decided cases; the role of military leader will emerge in the unfolding story. The most frequent responsibility of a prophet, of course, was to convey something of God's will or plan to the people. In verse 6 we see Deborah in this second role. She summons an

Israelite named Barak and announces that God instructs him to take troops and go to a place where God will give Barak a victory over General Sisera and his chariot-army. Is Barak to be the deliverer?

Barak replies (v. 8) that he will undertake the mission only if Deborah accompanies him. Deborah agrees but warns that Sisera will be overcome by a woman, not by Barak. Who then will be the deliverer? At this point the reader may well suppose that the woman deliverer will be Deborah. So Barak summons the troops, and Deborah accompanies him to the designated battle site.

Verse 11 offers some parenthetical information necessary for the rest of the story. A man named Heber the Kenite has encamped with his family in the neighborhood of the battle scene. Heber is identified as a descendant of Moses' father-in-law; this important fact puts readers on notice that these Kenites are related by marriage to the Israelites rather than to the Canaanites.

Sisera comes out to fight (v. 12), and Deborah commands Barak to attack. At God's initiative the Canaanite army goes into a panic and flees. Barak pursues the main force, who are slain to the last soldier. One would think that Barak might qualify as deliverer for this accomplishment; but General Sisera has dismounted from his chariot and fled away on foot, so the enemy is not yet destroyed.

Sisera flees (v. 17) directly to the encampment of Heber the Kenite, the man who was introduced in verse 11. It seems a good choice, for "there was peace" between Heber and King Jabin of the Canaanites for whom Sisera is General (v. 17). Heber has allied himself with the Canaanites, not with his Israelite relatives. Sisera goes to the tent of Heber's wife Jael, who invites him in, gives him a drink of milk, and covers him. He asks her to stand guard as he sleeps, but instead she kills him by driving a tent peg into his head. Barak arrives to see the result of Jael's action; Deborah's word that Sisera will fall by the hand of a woman is fulfilled.

Chapter 5 records the so-called Song of Deborah, which is thought to be one of the oldest pieces preserved in the Hebrew Bible and probably considerably older than the prose story of chapter 4. The song is sung by both Deborah and Barak (v. 1), offering an alternative and poetic version of the events of chapter 4. There are fairly obvious inconsistencies and variations in detail between the two chapters, although most commentators concur that parts of the poem are very obscure. The opening sections seem to celebrate the new era of prosperity for the Israelite "peasantry" because of the leadership of Deborah, who "arose as a mother in Israel" (v. 7). Verses 12–18 review the muster of the tribes for battle under Barak's leadership. According to the poem, many Israelite tribes participate who are not included in chapter 4. In the description of the battle itself (vv. 19–23) a different location is given, and the forces of nature participate in accomplishing the victory (vv. 20–21).

Sisera's death by the hand of Jael is recited in verses 24–27. Some aspects of the poetic account do match the prose story of chapter 4: the giving of milk to drink instead of water, the detail of the tent peg and the hammer, and the piercing of Sisera's head appear in both versions. But the poem differs significantly from the prose version in other details: (1) Jael does not invite Sisera into her tent; (2) Sisera does not sleep; there is no covering; and (3) an explicit positive value is placed on Jael's action: "Most blessed of women be Jael, the wife of Heber the Kenite, of tent-dwelling women most blessed" (v. 24). The prose has no comparable evaluation of Jael's action.

The poem of chapter 5 then turns to a scene not mentioned in the prose. In the home of Sisera, his mother peers through the window wondering why he is delayed, to which the answer is given, "are they not finding and dividing the spoil?"(v. 30)—girls for the soldiers and fine clothing for the women to whom they will return.

Even in such a brief summation of the biblical material, ethically disturbing aspects of the story are apparent. Among the more egregiously offensive themes for many readers are the total annihilation of enemy forces, killing a sleeping person, and women as spoils of war.

On the other hand, the story contains aspects that offer promise toward models for the role of women in public life. Examples may include a woman as judge deciding disputes and as prophet conveying God's word, a woman and a man in partnership, and women participating in the deliverance of oppressed people.

Feminist biblical interpretation and also newer literary approaches have demonstrated both theoretically and practically that aspects of any story can be viewed in either a positive or a negative light, and that even the same verses often point different readers in different directions. In such cases differing responses to the biblical text may each carry some important word to us as we relate a scriptural text to our own situations. The remainder of this chapter seeks to illustrate the helpfulness of multiple responses by bringing together insights of some Asian and Western women interpreters.

Judges 4—5 is about a battle, a war scene, and moreover, a battle planned and commanded by God for defeat of the Canaanite King Jabin's army. As I try to let word-of-God come alive for me in interpreting this story, I begin by recognizing that I do not like this basis for the story here or almost anywhere else it appears in the Bible. I believe war is generally a bad way for human beings to "settle" their differences, and the biblical imagery of God as planner or promulgator of battles seems to me potentially dangerous in that it may reinforce among Christians some too-easy acceptance of the appropriateness of war. This problem is frequently raised by my students, and it is surely one of the most difficult aspects of biblical interpretation. Many shades of opinion on the question of just war or types of pacifism continue to be represented within the Christian community. Without any pretense of giving full consideration to this issue, let me make two observations.

First, the story in Judges 4—5 is about overcoming an enemy to bring to an end a long period of oppression. As a white North American, I have not experienced this situation. The discussion of military or guerrilla options that surely takes place among persons in such situations of militarily enforced systemic oppression has not been a part of my life and world. My life is not like that of Koreans under Japanese occupation or Filipino or other peoples under a dictatorship. The choices facing Bonhoeffer and others concerning the Hitler regime have not been forced on me. I suspect that I am inconsistent in my ethical evaluation of uprisings in various parts of our 1990s globe, and I know that I make my assessments with very limited and filtered knowledge of the actual circumstances.

Second, in any such oppressive situation, the oppression itself must be named as a form of violence perpetrated by those who are in control. We are able to recognize this violence (sometimes) when it results in outright deaths, as in the many lynchings of blacks in past generations in the United States. But we know in hindsight that even such violence was often nonreported, underreported, or publicly justified by blaming its victims. The violence may often be less direct, in the form of intimidation or lack of access to resources that results in, for instance, malnutrition or un- or underemployment. Again, by my very existence as a well-educated and well-employed white North American, I am in some way complicit in such a structure both locally and globally. It is inevitably difficult for the one who is complicit in or who benefits from a given structure to evaluate neutrally or fairly the strategies for its transformation, let alone its overthrow. These observations about the context of oppression, the violent nature of oppression, and my own social location provide the necessary backdrop for considering the possibilities and problems of relating the roles of Deborah and Jael to the concerns of contemporary women in various cultural contexts.

Deborah: Prophet and Judge

We turn first to Deborah, prophet and judge. Deborah stands alongside three other Old Testament women in her designation as prophet: Miriam (Ex. 15:20), Huldah (2 Kings 22:14), and Noadiah (Neh. 6:4). Although female prophets mentioned in scripture are few in number compared with named male prophets, the range of texts and descriptions suggests a continuing prophetic function for women in ancient Israel. Thus Deborah's calling to convey God's word to Barak need not be regarded as unique.

She is portrayed as a woman of authority because she conveys a word from God.

As judge, Deborah is described initially as overseeing cases at a regular time and place. In this capacity, too, she is depicted as a woman of authority.[1] Then, at Barak's insistence, she accompanies him to the battle. The reason for Barak's request is not given by the narrator, nor is Deborah's role at the battle elaborated. It seems clear, however, that Barak thought Deborah's presence would in some way assure the promised victory. In the other stories of deliverance from oppression in the book of Judges, a male leader is center stage; but here, with Deborah's initiative and accompanying presence, there is a different picture.

Given the military context, many readers consciously or unconsciously view Deborah as an "honorary male." In much of the literature of the ancient world, and also in the psyche of much of contemporary North America, war and battle are so exclusively the domain of males that females cannot participate except as honorary members of the male group. Barak, then, is somehow humiliated or viewed as less of a man because he asks for a woman's help, so that his opportunity for glory is taken away from him. If the story thus functions only to validate women in combat, without raising questions about combat per se, then in my view we risk taking a step backward.

Yet perhaps there is a possibility in the text and in our response to it that can point a way through this dilemma: to the extent that the male is humiliated by the women's warring acts; to the extent that when we read this story, killing seems less acceptable when initiated by women; perhaps to that extent all of us are summoned by this biblical narrative to examine why we do not regard killing as equally reprehensible when done by men. Perhaps by pressing on us that question, the work of Deborah and Jael can lead us toward dismantling our too-easy acceptance of the structural violence of warfare. It is with that possibility in view that we may consider some other angles of vision on Deborah, angles that move beyond the specific context of warfare.

Some Filipino women, for instance, noted the unusualness of Barak's request that Deborah accompany him and suggested that this entire narrative be studied under the rubric of male-female cooperation. Deborah's comment about Sisera falling by the hand of a woman, and the eventual outcome of the story, helped the Filipino group to develop this theme of partnership, in contrast to the concept of Barak's humiliation by female participation.

Another way of looking at the story concentrates on Deborah as the authority figure offering decisions and divine instruction and asks after the nature of that authority of a woman to which even the man (Barak) is obedient. Among some Korean women there is an effort to extol Deborah's leadership without compromising Barak's role. In a context where ordination of women is rare among the larger Presbyterian denominations, some groups have sought to include Deborah as a biblical example supporting the concept of women's ordination to religious leadership. Those opposing this position have argued that the example of Deborah is inadmissible because they view her leadership as occasional and charismatic, called up by God just for a certain occasion, whereas the leadership of ordained persons is for life in a routinized rather than charismatic mode.

Of course, this is only one tiny corner of a debate in a Korean denomination where women's ordination was voted down annually every year for fifty years in a row. Only in 1995 was the door formally opened for those women who see themselves in Deborah's train. The point is that a question that may seem trivial to some readers, the question of whether there were diverse kinds of judges in early Israel (routinized and/or charismatic) and which kind Deborah was, makes a great deal of existential difference to Christians elsewhere. Those focusing on Deborah's appearance as limited to this battle story claim that she cannot serve as a model for ongoing leadership; those who concentrate on verse 5 and regular adjudication of cases see Deborah in quite a different light. In sum, despite the military context that may give us pause, Deborah may be seen as a model for women in authority in the religious sphere and as a model for cooperation between women and men.

Jael

The second key woman of this story, Jael, is involved in an action that is wrenchingly difficult for many readers. However we deal with her story, we need to note that the poetic text calls Jael blessed, and we need to consider what that may mean in the context of the poetic version of the event.

On a first level, Jael is surely celebrated as blessed simply because she killed the enemy general. In this way she is remembered positively even as are the women of Filipino or Korean or other cultures who have done a courageous act, even killing, for the freedom of their people. From an androcentric (male-centered) perspective, the blessing of Jael taunts the enemy Canaanites by recalling that their great military leader was killed by a woman. She has humiliated the enemy Sisera and his people.

At a deeper level, however, Jael's killing of Sisera can be read as a rejection of rape, or a protest against rape, especially rape of women victims of war. Both in psychological theory and in our common knowledge of behavior of armies, sex and violence are closely intertwined. A number of scholars, both women and men, have recently suggested that these dimensions are at work in the story of Jael. My interpretation will follow especially the proposals of Susan Niditch and Ann Wansbrough.[2]

Much traditional scholarship has suggested that Jael violated the sacred rules of Near Eastern hospitality to guests by her violence against Sisera. By this ancient custom, which is still preserved in some areas today, the host was responsible not only for entertaining guests but also for their protection. It should be noted that this emphasis on hospitable protection can be much more easily related to the prose text, in which Jael invites Sisera into her tent, than to the poetic version, in which the circumstances of Sisera's presence are not specified. Wansbrough points out, however, that within the hospitality system a male guest would ordinarily be received by a male host, in areas of the encampment open to males. We do not know a great deal about living arrangements in extended families of ancient Israel, but reference to the tent of Jael can be interpreted to mean that Sisera entered "women's quarters," properly off limits for male guests.[3] Sisera asks for a drink (in both prose and poem) and for protection (only in the prose), but Jael may well have anticipated rape.

Whether or not Sisera entered restricted quarters, the poetic language used in describing his death is full of sexual overtones. The principal clue is the appearance of the word *feet* (NRSV; Hebrew *raglaim*) in 5:27. The NRSV translation pictures Sisera on the ground at Jael's feet (literally). But Hebrew certainly knows an alternative, euphemistic meaning of the word *feet* as genitals. And the Hebrew word also can mean *legs*. Hence Niditch, Wansbrough, and others translate *between her legs* (with clear sexual overtones) rather than *at her feet*. Niditch renders the key verse as follows:

> Between her legs he knelt, he fell, he lay
> Between her legs he knelt, he fell
> Where he knelt, there he fell, despoiled.[4]

Niditch has shown that the vocabulary for kneeling (NRSV, "sank"), lying (NRSV, "lay still"), and despoiling (NRSV, "dead") all appear both in contexts of death and in sexual contexts, often of sexual betrayal.[5] Given that all these words in the verse are capable of double meaning in relation to sex and death, it seems reasonable to read the poem with this double meaning in view. Sisera, who in usual circumstances would be the potential rapist, the aggressor, the one who may kill when he is finished with the woman, is instead pictured in the role and posture of the woman who seeks with supplication and turning to ward off her rapist. Jael, who in usual circumstances would be the supplicant and victim, is pictured in the role and posture of initiator, victor, perhaps we must say aggressor. So although the poem taunts Sisera's people with the report of his death at the hands of a woman, it does so in a way that says "no" to rape in the context of war.

In the 1990s it would be difficult to pretend that rape in the context of war is an ancient problem. The news media have made it impossible for us to remain innocent of the fate of so-called noncombatants. Recent reports from Bosnia-Herzegovina of the hundreds of women raped by enemy soldiers—sometimes gang raped or raped repeatedly to ensure that they would become pregnant, then abandoned—are but one recent example.

The news stories about Korean, Filipino, and other "comfort women" who are seeking reparations from the Japanese government offer yet another prominent example. These women, now ages 65–80, were captured or kidnapped and forced to become "sex slave" prostitutes for the Japanese army during World War II. During my time in Japan, I met Japanese women who were supporting the efforts of those Korean women. And in Korea, I had the privilege of participating in a worship service with ten of these women and a dozen other Korean women who are supporting their appeal. Early in the service, each host woman chose a comfort woman as her honorary grandmother, and there was a time for sharing of stories in pairs. Tears began to fall; hands, arms, and shoulders were clasped together; and translation fell by the wayside for me and the one other American woman present. We did learn that one woman, married over forty years, had never revealed her story to her husband. At the conclusion of worship, a traditional Korean drum was brought out, and the older women led the younger generation in traditional dancing and singing, punctuated by fits of laughter. It is for such healing that the anti-rape reading of the story of Jael is given. It is against such rape and against the creation of more such brokenness that the story of Jael must be comprehended as anti-rape and told with boldness.

Sisera's Mother

It is also essential to note that there are more women in the poem. In the stanza immediately following the lines about Jael we read of Sisera's mother who wonders why her son is delayed (vv. 28–30). Early in the poem (v. 7), Deborah is praised as "mother in Israel" for her public role of leadership; now at the end the poet gives us a glimpse of Sisera's mother in the private sphere of her home, gazing out through the latticed window and saying: "Why is his chariot so long in coming? Why tarry the hoofbeats of his chariots?" She and her wise women attendants give answer. Of course, the soldiers are collecting more booty: fancy clothing for us and "a girl or two for every man." (The Hebrew says, literally, "a *womb* or two.") Surely this line confirms the reading of Jael's action as anti-rape. The poem and its singers are well aware that rape is part of the traditional aftermath of victory. Plundering is also well known, not just collecting of baubles of war souvenirs, but also the despoiling of economic and natural resources of the defeated area. Although this poem is clearly intended as a taunt song against Canaan, readers distant from the emotions of that ancient battle almost always feel empathy for Sisera's mother as she rationalizes his delay. We hear the catch in her voice, the anguish of every mother who waits at home. No mother should have to lose a child. I do not think that feeling of empathy is wrong, yet again my Korean sisters have helped me to gain a broader perspective.

Conclusion

I conclude with this story. A group of Korean women were expressing some enthusiasm for Jael's exploits, and I commented that most women I knew—white, middle/upper-class North Americans like me—had trouble with this story. I suggested certain roots for our difficulties with the story: we are too accustomed to having women on a pedestal protected by men, and we are too accustomed to not having to defend our homeland. Many of us are also influenced by the Christian theme of "turning the other cheek." I asked these Koreans what they could offer out of their setting that might be of help to me. After a brief pause, there came a bold reply from the far end of the table. "If you American women would just realize that your place in this story is with Sisera's mother, waiting to collect the spoil of your interventions across the world . . ." I did not want to hear that. I did not want to be reminded of the negative effects of first-world colonialism and military might in which I participate by my citizenship. But as I have reflected longer about it, I wonder whether I did not hear God's prophet as that woman spoke. That thought and that exchange remain among the most disturbing and the most profound moments of my Asian journey, a time of hearing the Bible as word of God through the voices of those not like myself.

Notes

1. See Danna Nolan Fewell, "Judges," in *The Women's Bible Commentary*, ed. Carol A. Newsom and Sharon H. Ringe (Louisville: Westminster/John Knox Press, 1992), 69.
2. Ann Wansbrough, "Blessed Be Jael Among Women: For She Challenged Rape," in *Women of Courage: Asian Women Reading the Bible*, ed. Lee Oo Chung et al. (Seoul, Korea: Asian Women's Resource Centre for Culture and Theology, 1992), 101–22; Susan Niditch, "Eroticism and Death in the Tale of Jael," in *Gender and Difference in Ancient Israel*, ed. P. L. Day (Minneapolis: Fortress Press, 1989), 43–57.
3. Wansbrough, "Blessed Be Jael," 110.
4. Niditch, "Eroticism and Death," 47.
5. Ibid., 48–49.

3

Dangerous Seductress or Elusive Lover?
The Woman of Ecclesiastes 7

The Bible is to be interpreted in the light of its witness to God's work of reconciliation in Christ. The Scriptures, given under the guidance of the Holy Spirit, are nevertheless the words of men, conditioned by the language, thought forms, and literary fashions of the places and times at which they were written. They reflect views of life, history, and the cosmos which were then current. The church, therefore, has an obligation to approach the Scriptures with literary and historical understanding.
—The Confession of 1967

E cclesiastes 7:26–29 is a veritable testimony to the truth of the above statements from The Confession of 1967. This difficult portion of scripture has come to us in human words—in this case, literally, the "words of men"—not only in its original form, but also in its transmission and its interpretation. Without attention to the literary and historical contexts, one may justly conclude that these verses contain nothing more than the gratuitous remarks of one who has only contempt for women. Such an understanding of the passage is reflected in the rendering of the New English Bible:

The wiles of a woman I find mightier than death; her heart is a trap to catch you and her arms are fetters. The man who is pleasing to God may escape her, but she will catch a sinner. "See," says the Speaker, "this is what I have found, reasoning things out one by one, after searching long without success: I have found one man in a thousand worth the name, but I have not found one woman among them all."

Every translation is necessarily an interpretation, and this one is no exception.[1] It seems clear that the translators of the New English Bible thought that the text has to do with women in general—any woman. This view is also found in the Jerusalem Bible: "I find woman more bitter than death; she is a snare, her heart a net, her arms are chains."[2] Other translations, however, identify the problem to be not women in general, but only certain kinds

23

of women. So the New International Version reads: "I find more bitter than death the woman who is a snare, whose heart is a trap and whose hands are chains" (similarly New Revised Standard Version, New American Bible, New American Standard Bible). In this view, the author has a negative judgment only of a certain woman, usually thought to be an adulteress or a prostitute.[3] Occasionally, commentators speculate that the author's misogynistic attitude has been formed by his bitter experiences with a particular woman, either his wife or his mother. Thus, Frank Zimmerman imagines that the author of Ecclesiastes had become impotent and harbored deep resentment toward his wife and mother and, consequently, toward women in general.[4]

Yet the sudden attention to any woman at all would make little sense within the larger literary context (Eccl. 7:15–29). Up to this point, the issue in this passage seems to be the impossibility of a righteousness and a wisdom that will avert death. As far as righteousness is concerned, "there is no one on earth so righteous, who does only good and does not err" (v. 20, my translation). As for wisdom, Ecclesiastes says he found it utterly unfathomable and inaccessible (7:23–25). The theme of wisdom's inaccessibility would continue in 8:1–17, a passage about the elusiveness of wisdom and knowledge in the face of the problems that mortals confront in an arbitrary world: "Who is so wise? Who knows the solution of anything?" (8:1, my translation). Hence, if the comments in 7:25–29 are merely about the character of women, as it is commonly assumed, they are completely out of place.

The Wicked Seductress

Significantly, the language used to describe wisdom's elusiveness in verses 23–24 is reminiscent of the depiction of the elusive ideal woman of Proverbs 31, who is the embodiment of personified Wisdom. According to Proverbs 31:10, that ideal woman is also difficult to find ("who can find?"), and her worth is beyond (*rāḥôq*, literally, "far [from]") jewels. This elusive woman is an image of Wisdom herself, for elsewhere it is said that one who *finds* Wisdom will find her to be more precious than jewels (Prov. 3:13–18).[5] For Ecclesiastes, too, ideal wisdom is inaccessible: "All this I have tested by wisdom. I said, 'I would be wise,' but that is beyond me (*rěḥôqâ mimmenî*). All that happens is inaccessible (*rāḥôq*) and utterly unfathomable; who can find it?" (vv. 23–24, my translation).

The author mixes metaphors, however. Ecclesiastes uses not only the idioms of a lover's pursuit (seeking and finding/not finding) but also the language of commerce, for he equates his quest for wisdom with accounting: "to seek wisdom and accounting, to know wickedness to be foolishness and folly to be irrationality" (v. 25, my translation). The word "accounting" is a commercial term widely found in the Near East, often in reference to economic documents like a ledger or an inventory. The image conjured up for the reader, then, is that of a merchant or an accountant poring over some business document, trying to account for every item, perhaps trying to assign everything to its appropriate place on a ledger and then to tally it all up in order to arrive at the balance. That is the kind of wisdom of which the author speaks—a wisdom that seeks to account for all discrepancies and explain all irregularities. The "merchant" or "accountant" in this case tries to distinguish wisdom from folly, as if each can clearly be assigned to either side of a ledger. But the author recognizes that it is an impossible task to sort out such details, as one might attempt to do with an economic document. No one is so wise as to sort out these universal problems (see also 8:1, "Who is so wise? Who knows the solution to anything?" [my translation]).

It is precisely in this context—with its allusion to someone checking a business document and attempting to distinguish wisdom from folly—that Ecclesiastes says, "and I find more bitter than death is the woman, inasmuch as she is a snare, her heart is a net, her hands are fetters" (my translation). This is surely not a polemic against womankind in general. Nor is it a barb directed at a specific woman or a particular type of woman. The text speaks literally of "the woman" (with the definite article in Hebrew), as if the reader ought to know who that "woman" is. In the immediate context, the most likely referent is "folly," a feminine noun in Hebrew and the only noun in the preceding verse marked by the definite article. This is apparently the understanding of the Greek translators, arguably the earliest interpreters of the text on record.[6] This conclusion is all the more compelling when one realizes that the language in verse 26 echoes the teachings in conventional wisdom about the "strange woman," a dangerous seductress who lures one away from Wisdom's loving and protective embrace. In Proverbs 1—9, this deadly seductress stands in contrast to Wisdom; she is the "other woman," a personification of Folly.

Such a portrayal of the seductress is quite typical of the wider wisdom tradition of the ancient Near East, as commentators have duly noted. In the Egyptian wisdom text called *The Instruction of Anii,* this dangerous one is seen as a foreign woman, a wanton adulteress who is ready to pounce on the innocent youngster: "She waits to ensnare you, a great deadly wrongdoing when one hears of it."[7] In the Wisdom of Ben Sira, the pernicious woman is described in a similar way: "Do not go to meet a loose woman, lest you fall into her snares" (Sir. 9:3); "A harlot is regarded as spittle // A married woman is a deadly trap to those who embrace her" (Sir. 26:22, my translation). In Proverbs 5:4–5, the dangerous seductress, who is the embodiment of Folly, is described thus:

[B]ut in the end she is bitter as wormwood,
  sharp as a two-edged sword.
Her feet go down to death;
  her steps follow the path to Sheol.

Similar images of this femme fatale are found in Proverbs 2:16–19; 5:20; 6:24–35; 7:5–27; 9:13–18; 23:27–28. This is a "woman" who is relentless in her seduction and deadly in her pursuit. To biblical scholar Norbert Lohfink, then, these words in Ecclesiastes are clichés about women in a patriarchal society.[8] Yet dangerous men also entice, trap, and otherwise lead one away from the influence of Wisdom (see Prov. 1:10–19; 2:12–15;[9] 6:1–5; compare Ps. 140:1–5), and one's own wickedness and folly are described in similar ways (Prov. 5:22–23; 12:13). So these are not strictly clichés about women; they are, rather, clichés about the threat of folly and wickedness. Nevertheless, it is true that the deadly seductress, representing Folly, is most frequently portrayed in the Bible as a woman, the "other woman." As such she is set over against another female figure, Wisdom, the one who protects and watches and gives life (Prov. 1:20–33; 3:13–18; 4:5–13; 8:1–31; 9:1–18).

These two "women"—or two types of women—are symbolic of the tension between Wisdom and Folly, as is clear in Proverbs 9. One represents life, the other death; one represents righteousness, the other wickedness. The femme fatale in Israelite wisdom literature is not, therefore, an individual woman. Nor is she necessarily a specific type of woman, although she is usually portrayed as a foreign woman, an adulteress, or a prostitute. Rather, she is a composite image of Folly herself (Prov. 9:13–18). Folly is out on a hunt, as it were, trying to lure and trap people and lead them down the deadly path. She is as pernicious as the wicked men who threaten to swallow up the innocent like Sheol and who spread a net to trap their victims (Prov. 1:10–19; compare Ps. 140:1–5). This is the "woman" of whom the author of Ecclesiastes speaks in 7:26. Folly is out looking for her prey, and she is dangerous in her wiles. She is more bitter than death itself.[10] According to our text, the one who is fortunate (literally, "the one who is *good* before God") will be able to escape her, but the one who errs (*hote'*), the bungler, will be captured by her (v. 26; see also Prov. 5:22–23).[11] Yet the author probably means that in reality no one will escape this dangerous "woman," because "there is no human on earth who is righteous, who does only good and does not err" (v. 20, my translation). No one escapes the deadly snare of this dangerous "other woman."

The Elusive Lover

The text in 7:27 continues the idea of a quest for an accounting, an idea first broached in verse 25: "See what I have found, says Qohelet, one by one to find an accounting" (my translation).[12] Like a merchant or an accountant, the author runs down the imaginary business document item by item ("one by one"), hoping to find an explanation for apparent discrepancies that he sees. Obviously, "the account" is troubling him; the solution is eluding him. Something, it seems, requires an explanation.

So far the narrative makes sense. But suddenly we find an odd remark in verse 28b: "One man among a thousand I found, but a woman among all these I have not found." The text is, at best, elliptical. Most commentators presume the author to be saying that there is one *reliable* or *capable* man in a thousand, or that there is a rare friend who is true,[13] but there is no equivalent woman among all these. Here again one notes the interpretive nature of translations, as many try to make up for the apparent ellipsis. Thus the New International Version has: "I found one *upright* man among a thousand, but not one *upright* woman" (emphasis added) and the Revised English Bible reads: "I have found one man in a thousand *worthy to be called upright,* but I have not found one woman among them all" (emphasis added). In other words, a good man is extremely rare (only 0.1 percent of those searched!), but a good woman is nonexistent.

The statement is a notorious problem for the interpreter; it is especially problematic for anyone who wants to appropriate this passage as scripture. It is difficult to explain it as anything other than a misogynistic remark, although some scholars have proffered nonderogatory interpretations or insisted that Qohelet is quoting a well-known attitude only to reject it.[14]

From a sociohistorical standpoint, such a negative assessment of women in Israel during the postexilic period (period in which the book of Ecclesiastes was composed) does not come as a surprise.[15] The Israelites who returned to their homeland after years in exile found themselves to be a minority in an alien environment, surrounded by people of various ethnic, cultural, and religious backgrounds who had already tried to establish their claims in the land. Nothing less than the survival of their community was at stake, for the former exiles faced the temptation of assimilation into their new environment and, through exogamy (marriage outside the ethnic/national group), the prospect of losing their legal claim to property.[16] Consequently, marriages to men or women outside the community were forbidden. But as was typical in that time and place, it was the women who bore most of the blame and the brunt of the polemics: The community had become "polluted" all because of the foreign women in its midst (see Ezra 9:2). Hence, some in the community, like Ezra, Nehemiah, and Malachi, called for the banishment of foreign wives or otherwise warned against foreign women (Ezra 9—10; Neh. 13:23–27; Mal. 2:10–16). At the same time, however, there were stories told in that period of heroic women, like Ruth and Esther—the former, a foreign woman; the latter, a native savior of her people. In the androcentric (male-centered) culture of ancient Israel, women became metaphors for both the negative and positive influences in society. They represented either what was salutary (the virtuous wife) or what was unsavory (the "other woman"). They were symbolic of what people should seek or shun. In such a world, women were either elusive virtuous brides or aggressive and deadly seductresses.

That same tension between the two types of women, representing Wisdom and Folly, is found in the book of Proverbs, which was probably assembled also during the Persian period. Thus, in the rhetoric of Proverbs 1—9, Folly is depicted in terms of the dangerous "other" woman, the outsider, whereas Wisdom is portrayed as the good wife on whom one may always rely. Evidently, in antiquity, as in modern times, men are wont to view women in terms of caricatured personifications of virtue or vice.[17]

So in this context, a misogynistic remark in Ecclesiastes would not have been surprising. Nevertheless, this saying in verse 28b seems intrusive. The passage is, after all, not about women at all. The sudden polemic is out of place, for the passage seems to be concerned with the dangers of Folly and the elusiveness of Wisdom, as we see in verses 22–27. Moreover, the use of the Hebrew word 'ādām for "man" as opposed to "woman" is out of character for Ecclesiastes. In forty-eight other instances in the book, 'ādām refers to a human being (as opposed to animals or the deity) or to any person ("anyone, someone"). When a specific person is meant, the author uses the word 'îš. Certainly in contrast to "woman" one expects 'îš instead of 'ādām. The uncharacteristic usage of 'ādām in verse 28b is all the more striking when one notes that 'ādām is used in the very next verse (v. 29), and there it clearly refers to all humanity, because the pronoun that follows is the plural "they." In terms of logic, too, verse 28b contradicts verse 29: "One man among a thousand I have found, but I have not found a woman among all these. *Only*, see what I have found . . . " (my translation). The word *only* at the beginning of verse 29 makes little sense in its present context, because verse 28b already identifies what has been found, namely, the rare "one man." If one omits verse 28b, however, one would not miss a beat: "The one whom I have sought still, I have not found. Only, see what I have found: that God has made humanity just right, but they have sought many inventions" (my translation). For all these reasons, then, I would submit that verse 28b has been secondarily inserted. One may surmise that this interpolation comes probably from the hand of a copyist who misunderstood the allusion to the dangerous "woman" in verse 26. Thinking that the passage was meant to be an indictment of women in general or of a particular type of woman (and not of personified Folly), the copyist added what may have been intended as an illustration of the point of the passage. It was perhaps an ancient sexist joke. This marginal comment, unfortunately, was later incorporated into the body of the text, thereby skewing the meaning of the passage.

The adverb *still* in verse 28a ("the one whom I have sought *still*"), in fact, suggests that the search is not new. One is prompted to ask what it is that the author *still* "seeks" and cannot find, and one is led back to the same verb *seek* in verse 25: "to seek wisdom and accounting" (my translation). We cannot, therefore, separate the interpretation of verse 28 from verses 23–25, which concerns the search for ideal wisdom. Furthermore, it is not amiss to observe that the motif of seeking and finding/not finding is at home in the language of courtship (see especially Song of Sol. 3:1–6; 5:6; 6:1; Hos. 2:7). In the wisdom tradition, the elusive lover may be Woman Wisdom herself. According to the sages, the one who is able to find Wisdom "finds" life and obtains divine favor (Prov. 8:35; compare also Prov. 18:22), but the one who misses the mark—the one who errs—in the search will be in mortal danger (Prov. 8:36; Sir. 6:27; compare Eccl. 7:26). For those who so err, Wisdom will be particularly inaccessible: "Then they will call upon me, but I will not answer; they will *seek* me diligently, but will not *find* me" (Prov. 1:28, emphasis mine). One who is able to "find Wisdom," then, is said to be fortunate indeed, for Wisdom is more unattainable than jewels (Prov. 3:13–15).

The language is reminiscent of the description of the consummate wise woman, who symbolizes Wisdom and who is said to be difficult to find and more unattainable than jewels (Prov. 31:10). That is the same language that we find in 7:24 of the author's quest to understand all that is going on in the world. Hence, it seems clear that Wisdom, specified as the quest for an accounting (v. 25), is also the intended object in verse 28. The elusiveness and inaccessibility of Wisdom are at issue here, not the relative character of women and men.

Thus, verses 25b–26 are balanced by verses 27–28a. The former concerns Folly; the latter concerns Wisdom. It appears, however, that in the end neither Folly nor Wisdom is a real option for anyone: the one is deadly, but the other is elusive. It is in such a crazy game of hide-and-seek that human beings find themselves. They are pursued persistently by Folly, a pernicious seductress and hunter from whom they must try to escape but cannot, even as they try desperately to find the one who will keep them safe, who will protect them from all dangers—Wisdom. But this Wisdom—the ideal "woman"—eludes them. Wisdom will not save the poor, desperate mortal.

Finally, the author concludes, as at the end of the preceding literary unit (7:12–14), by calling attention to what God has done. One is asked to "see" the one thing that the author has discovered (7:29), namely, what God has done, even as one is asked in 7:13–14 to "see" what God has done—both the good and the bad in the world. According to our text, God has made human beings "just right" (Hebrew *yāšār*), literally "balanced" or "level."

The reference to the "balanced" character of mortals harks back to the beginning of the literary unit (7:15–18). It appears that the author is making the point that is made at the beginning of the literary unit—that one must avoid the hubris of thinking that wisdom and righteousness will allow one to avert destruction. Ecclesiastes advises:

Do not be exceedingly righteous and do not show yourself excessively wise, lest you be confounded. Do not be exceedingly wicked and do not be a fool, lest you die before your time. It is good that you grasp the one but also not let go of the other, for the one who fears God goes forth with both of them. (7:16–18; my translation)

Ecclesiastes warns against overconfidence in wisdom and righteousness. Indeed, he argues that one who fears God will come to terms with the fact that mortals can, at best, proceed in life with wisdom/righteousness on the one hand and folly/wickedness on the other.[18] The one who fears God would not presume to be secure in righteousness, "for there is no human so righteous, who does only good and does not err" (v. 20, my translation). By the same token, no one must presume to be protected by Wisdom, for she is as unattainable as the elusive ideal woman. Instead, every human being is inevitably endangered by the deadly traps of the "other woman," Folly, for everyone who errs—and that is every human being—is caught by her (v. 26).

Beyond Male-Centered Metaphors

There can be no denying that the language and images in Ecclesiastes 7:26–29 are male centered; the text is written from a thoroughly male perspective. The original text was, indeed, "conditioned by the language, thought forms, and literary fashions" of its time and place. It was written in the postexilic period, and like other texts from that period is characterized by a tendency to use metaphors of women caricatured either as the pernicious seductress or as the heroic savior. We must name the problem here: that way of objectifying women is undeniably male centered. And that male-focused perspective of the author developed into a misogynistic one in the process of transmission, when the sexist interpretation of a copyist was somehow incorporated into the canon and then perpetuated in the history of interpretation.

Accordingly, in the third century C.E., Gregory Thaumaturgos interpreted these verses to be a warning against the wiles of *all* women. As John Jarick astutely observes, "It should not surprise us that a celibate Church Father—and particularly one who learned his Christianity from Origen, a man so concerned to avoid the snares and traps of women that he castrated himself—wants his (male) readers to be well aware of the dangerous nature of Woman."[19] In the history of interpretation, then, women have in various ways been "demonized" on the basis of these words in Ecclesiastes. Indeed, in medieval times this passage is cited as a scriptural sanction for attacks on women. Thus the fifteenth-century manual for witch-hunts, known as the *Malleus Maleficarum,* quotes this passage to justify the actions of the inquisitors against women.[20] In contrast to such an interpretation, Martin Luther's understanding of the passage is relatively enlightened.

He rejected categorically the view that the text engaged in a polemic against the female sex, arguing that it is merely against certain women—for him, in his time and place, domineering women who "want to prescribe for men even those matters that pertain to the governance of public affairs."[21]

The point of the passage is not about women, however. The women—one a deadly seductress and the other an elusive lover—are metaphors. They are culturally conditioned, male-centered, and even offensive metaphors. As such, they are merely broken vessels that may, nevertheless, contain "living water." The message in the entire passage is that mortals are not able to escape the snares of death by means of righteousness or wisdom. No human being is so righteous, who does only good and does not err (7:20); no one is so wise as to escape the snares of folly and wickedness (7:26). So one who fears God—that is, one who recognizes the proper place of humanity in relation to God—will go forth in life with the awareness of human limitations, knowing that a mortal must always accept the realities of both good and bad, both righteousness and wickedness, both wisdom and folly.

With distinct echoes to the first half of this passage (7:15–22), the apostle Paul argues in Romans 3: "there is none righteous" (Rom. 3:10; compare Eccl. 7:20); "no one (who) does good" (Rom. 3:12; compare Eccl. 7:20); "their mouth is full of curses and bitterness" (Rom. 3:14; compare Eccl. 7:21–22); "there is no fear of God before their eyes" (Rom. 3:18; compare Eccl. 7:18); and "all have missed the mark/erred/sinned" (Rom. 3:23; compare Eccl. 7:20). For Paul, it is the impossibility of righteousness among mortals that necessitates the righteousness of God by grace alone. Ecclesiastes 7:23–29 makes a point similar to that of 7:15–22. Just as perfect righteousness is an impossibility among human beings, so perfect wisdom is an impossibility. Hence, neither righteousness nor wisdom can save a person from death; we are inevitably caught in its snare.

Interpreting Ecclesiastes in the light of the Bible's "witness to God's work of reconciliation in Christ," the Christian reader of this book hears, like Paul, the possibility of salvation for all errant ones—neither by human righteousness *nor by wisdom,* but by the grace of God alone. In the human words of Ecclesiastes, despite the androcentric metaphors and a misogynistic gloss, one can nevertheless discern the Word of God. The text, after all, does point us to God's work of reconciliation in Christ.

Notes

The quote from The Confession of 1967, appearing at the beginning of this chapter, is taken from the Presbyterian Church (U.S.A.) *Book of Confessions,* 9.29.

1. One may note that the Hebrew text mentions neither "the wiles" in verse 26 nor the expression "worth the name" in verse 28, and it has "the

woman" instead of "one woman." Moreover, the translation "mightier," though possible, is unnecessary. Certainly, death is said to be bitter in 1 Samuel 15:32 and Sirach 41:1. Most important, in Proverbs 5:1–6 the femme fatale is said to be "bitter" as wormwood, and her feet descend to "death."

2. Accordingly, Leonard Swidler concludes: "This would seem to fulfill the definition of misogynism, of woman-hating," because in this text "*all* women have been reduced to essential evil." See his *Biblical Affirmations of Woman* (Philadelphia: Westminster Press, 1979), 128.

3. So the Targum takes the woman to be one "who causes her husband sorrow" and should, therefore, be divorced by her husband, lest he be "caught in her harlotry" (See Peter S. Knobel, "The Targum of Qohelet," in *The Aramaic Bible,* vol. 15 [Collegeville, Minn.: Liturgical Press, 1991], 41).

4. Frank Zimmerman, *The Inner World of Qohelet* (New York: KTAV, 1973), 29–30, 152.

5. On the relationship between the woman of Proverbs 31 and personified Wisdom in Proverbs 1–9, see Claudia Camp, *Wisdom and the Feminine in the Book of Proverbs,* Bible and Literature Series 11 (Sheffield, Eng.: Almond Press, 1985), 90–96.

6. The best Greek witnesses, including a recently published bilingual codex from the third century C.E., the Syro-Hexaplaric and Coptic versions, all indicate an accusative pronoun: "And I find *her.*" Most scholars regard the accusative pronoun to be a secondary addition. Yet the Greek translators of Ecclesiastes are very literalistic in their renderings; they do not tend to add for clarification.

7. See Miriam Lichtheim, *Ancient Egyptian Literature,* 3 vols. (Berkeley: University of California Press, 1971–80), 2:137.

8. Norbert Lohfink, *Kohelet,* Die neue echter Bibel (Würzburg: Echter Verlag, 1980), 57–58.

9. Structurally, according to the Hebrew text, Proverbs 2:12–15 parallels 2:16–19. The former concerns wicked men, the latter wicked women. Ironically, the New Revised Standard Version's inclusive language translation generalizes the offenders in verses 12–15, but the offender in verses 16–19 is gender specific: she is the "loose woman."

10. She is compared with death, even as wicked enticing men are compared with Sheol in Proverbs 1:10–19. Compare Proverbs 5:4–5, where death and Sheol are used synonymously.

11. The expressions "one who is good before God" and "one who errs" in Ecclesiastes (see also 2:26) simply refer to those who are lucky and those who are unlucky, respectively. These are not moral categories for the author. See H. L. Ginsberg, "The Structure and Contents of the Book of Koheleth," in *Wisdom in Israel and in the Ancient Near East,* Vetus Testamentum Supplement 3, ed. M. Noth and D. Winton Thomas (Leiden: E. J. Brill, 1969), 139.

12. *Qohelet* is the Hebrew name of the author that has been translated into Greek and Latin as *Ecclesiastes.*

13. See Diethelm Michel, *Untersuchungen zur Eigenart des Buches Qohelet,*

Beiheft zur Zeitschrift für die alttestamentliche Wissenschaft 183 (Berlin/New York: Walter de Gruyter, 1989), 231.

14. See, for example, Norbert Lohfink, "War Kohelet ein Frauenfeind? Ein Versuch, die Logik und den Gegenstand von Koh, 7, 23–8, 1a herauszufinden," in *La Sagesse de l'Ancien Testament,* Bibliotheca ephemeridum theologicarum lovanensium 51, ed. M. Gilbert (Leuven: Leuven University, 1979), 259–87, 417–20.

15. For the date and sociohistorical setting of Ecclesiastes, see C. L. Seow, "Linguistic Evidence and the Dating of Qohelet," *Journal of Biblical Literature* 115/4 (1996): 643–66; idem, "The Socioeconomic Context of 'the Preacher's' Hermeneutic," *The Princeton Seminary Bulletin,* n.s. 17/2 (1996): 168.

16. For this reconstruction of the sociohistorical setting, see Harold C. Washington, "The Strange Woman of Proverbs 1—9 and Post-Exilic Judaean Society," in *Second Temple Studies 2: Temple and Community in the Persian Period,* ed. T. C. Eskenazi and K. H. Richards (Sheffield, Eng.: JSOT Press, 1994), 207–32.

17. For a modern analogy to Proverbs 1—9, see Carol A. Newsom, "Woman and the Discourse of Patriarchal Wisdom: A Study of Proverbs 1—9," in *Gender and Difference in Ancient Israel,* ed. P. L. Day (Minneapolis: Augsburg Press, 1989), 142–60.

18. For the translation of Ecclesiastes 7:18, see Seow, "Socioeconomic Context," 192 n. 72.

19. John Jarick, *Gregory Thaumaturgos' Paraphrase of Ecclesiastes,* Society of Biblical Literature Septuagint and Cognate Studies 29 (Atlanta: Scholars Press, 1990), 188.

20. The manual was published in 1487 by two inquisitors, Heinrich Kramer and Jakob Sprenger, under the authority of Pope Innocent VIII. For examples of references to our text, Ecclesiastes, see Alan C. Kors and Edward Peters, *Witchcraft in Europe (1100–1700): A Documentary History* (Philadelphia: University of Pennsylvania Press, 1984), 126–27.

21. See his "Notes on Ecclesiastes," in *Luther's Works,* vol. 15, ed. Jaroslav Pelikan (St. Louis: Concordia Publishing), 130–31.

4

In Praise of Sophia:
The Witness of Tradition

Contemporary feminist theologians have raised and pressed the question of the appropriateness of theological language that is exclusively, predominantly, or even implicitly male centered. The vehemence of views expressed and the exuberance of accompanying innovations in worship, especially at the Re-imagining Conference of November 1993, have evoked a storm of protest from segments of the church. Feminist theologians often invoke the traditional Christian understanding of human beings as "created in the image and likeness of God" as justification for extrapolating from human, and specifically female-human, experience a better understanding of God. Over against this, it has been asserted that feminists put too great an emphasis on immanence, that their theologies are heretical or pagan, and that scripture and the traditional formulations of doctrines such as the Trinity, Christology, and atonement are incompatible with feminist theologies. A closer examination of the role of culture and human experience in the composition and reading of the Bible and in the formulation of these doctrines is thus central for an adjudication of these issues.

Such large and complex questions are too weighty to attempt to resolve in this chapter. Yet it is important to broach the subject of our language for God and to begin to bridge the growing rift in the church. It may be useful to draw the attention of contemporary Christians to two lessons from the Fathers of the church, the theologians of the first few centuries of the Christian era. First, the formulation of the fundamental doctrines of the Christian church took place within a particular cultural environment and to some degree under its influence. Second, there are precedents in the early church for dramatic use of female metaphors to describe God.

Rather than survey a range of Fathers who use such metaphors in their theological and devotional writings,[1] I will discuss Clement of Alexandria's use of Sophia/Wisdom imagery, as well as other female theological imagery, within the context of both his understanding of the relation of scripture to culture and his application of philosophical concepts of Logos/Word and other male theological imagery to Jesus as Savior. I focus on Clement, head of the catechetical school in Alexandria at the beginning of the third century, because he offers a sophisticated discussion of the theological criteria for appropriating cultural baggage in the very same writing as he offers some of the most striking patristic examples of female images applied to God. In other words, his use of graphic female imagery to speak of God is not the result of a careless and poorly considered use of notions widespread in a polytheistic environment. It is instead an integral part of his carefully constructed cultural hermeneutic.

Clement's Doctrine
of Christ the Logos

In his great tripartite work—the *Protreptikos, Paedagogos,* and *Stromateis*—Clement sets forth his doctrine of God, his formulation of the goal of human life, and the manner of reading scripture (and other sources) to discern the way to that goal.[2] Every aspect of Clement's theology is intimately related to his understanding of Jesus Christ as Logos/Sophia. Through this doctrine the essential elements of his Christian theology are connected with his culturally inclusive vision.

Clement's Logos doctrine stands at the confluence of the varied streams of his cultural world: Middle-Platonic philosophy,* Greco-Roman literature, Alexandrian Judaism, heterodox Gnosticism, and early Greek Christian apologetic traditions. At the same time, his vivid portrayal of the Logos as the Savior constitutes the personalizing vision and motivating force of his ethical and spiritual teaching. We will discuss this core doctrine by considering two broad questions. First, why is he persuaded that Middle-Platonic philosophy is compatible with Christianity? Second, how does he take the Logos of Middle Platonism and transform it into an instrument of Christian teaching?

Clement's Notion of a Philosophy
Compatible with Christ

Clement did not create his eclectic philosophical framework anew from bits and pieces selected from Plato, Aristotle, the Stoics, and neo-Pythagoreans. Instead, he incorporated his Christian beliefs into a Middle-

---

*Among the Middle Platonists, who flourished from about 50 B.C. to 200 A.D., Plato was considered to be the archetypical philosopher; the interpretation of his dialogues, especially the *Timaeus,* was at the center of their concerns. Yet they incorporated many Stoic and Aristotelian notions into their systems. For fuller explanation, see John Dillon, *The Middle Platonists,* rev. ed. (Ithaca, New York: Cornell University Press, 1996).

Platonic frame of reference, which was itself an eclectic construct. When Clement adopted this ready-made framework, he was not merely following the current vogue. He gives specific reasons for the compatibility of this philosophical framework to Christian teaching.

These guidelines constitute his answer to the question, Is Greek philosophy the "worldly wisdom" that, according to Paul, "is folly in God's eyes"? After emphasizing the need to trust in the power of God rather than to "glory in one's superiority in human intelligence," he argues that the "human tradition" rejected by Paul is restricted to those philosophies that deny the Creator and providence or have an inadequate notion of the spiritual nature of God—views he identifies as Epicurean and Stoic, respectively. Further, he notes: "The Word does not want the person of faith to be indifferent to truth and in fact lazy. For he says 'Seek and you shall find.'" The seeking leads to finding; that is, the seeker is led to Christ. Henceforth, believers are not forbidden to study philosophy but only to restrict themselves to "the sort of investigation that strengthens our faith."[3] He completes his argument by specifying the parameters of that sort of investigation:

> Teaching that follows Christ recognizes God in the Creator. It brings providence in, even to matters of detail. It shows that the elements are by nature subject to birth and change. It teaches us, so far as we can, to exercise our citizenship in likeness to God, and to accept God's plan as the directive power for the whole of our education.[4]

The first three criteria pertain to God's relation to the world. The first, that God must be recognized in the Creator, or more literally, that the "demiurge is to be deified," is clearly designed to assert firmly that the visible, material creation is neither accidental nor evil. Yet Clement phrases carefully to allow the delegated creative power posited in the Middle Platonist system.

Closely related is the second criterion, that a doctrine of providence is necessary, one that applies "even in matters of detail." Here, too, the ongoing divine presence and oversight are asserted. Yet study of the notion of providence throughout Clement's literary corpus shows that God's care is often mediated through natural law or in dealings with larger human communities.[5] Here he emphasizes that neither the philosophical, proto-scientific framework nor the broad historical working of providence excludes God's being the ultimate arbiter even of the minor details of an individual life.

The third criterion, closely related to both its precursors, specifies that the elements from which the material world is constituted began to exist at some moment in time and are liable to change. Here Clement's precise meaning has been the subject of debate. Certainly he rules out a material world without a Creator, and he excludes a world shaped from elements co-eternal with their Creator, but scholars differ on whether he teaches creation *ex nibilo* ("from nothing").[6] What is clear is his intention to assert that the forces of nature are subject to the power of the Creator.

In his final two criteria, Clement turns to the subject of the goal of human life and the path by which it is to be achieved. First, we are to "exercise our citizenship in likeness to God." Here we can recognize his oft-repeated characterization of the ultimate goal of the Christian life.[7] For gradual but steady ethical and spiritual transformation is the result of the Savior's teaching both for humankind as a whole and for the individual. Through this schooling in virtue the Christian is led first to the moderation of the passions, then to the achievement of *apatheia* (transcendence of the passions) and thence to the restoration of likeness to God and eventual participation in the very life of God.[8] Finally, in specifying that the divine plan is to be the highest authority in all instruction, Clement insists on a Christocentric interpretation of all reality, biblical and otherwise, for in the line just prior to the list of criteria, he alluded to the New Testament witness in precisely these terms. So his five criteria of a philosophy compatible with Christian belief may be summarized as follows: It must recognize God as Creator and Providential Ruler, and it must recognize that humans are called to become like God by accepting education according to the divine plan declared and enacted by the Savior.

Clement's Transformed Vision
of the Logos

This brings us to the second question, How does Clement take the Middle-Platonic Logos and transform it into an instrument of Christian teaching?

The Savior as the New, Liberating Orpheus

Our acceptance of the ethical and spiritual education according to the divine plan declared and enacted by the Savior, who is the Logos, is precisely the goal of Clement's great tripartite work. Fully revealed in Jesus, Christ as Logos also plays the broader role of implanting truth in all human beings. This notion, vividly portrayed, dominates Clement's *Protreptikos*. Here it is the Savior, the Logos, who sings a powerful new song:

> Behold the might of the new song! It has made humans out of stones, humans out of beasts. Those who were as dead, not being partakers of the true life, have come to life again, simply by becoming listeners to this song.[9]

Christ both sings and embodies the new song.[10] At the heart of Clement's theology is his conviction that the same one who "was in the beginning," the same Word of God through whom the universe came to exist, this very Word has now appeared to human beings, He alone being both, both God and human—the Author of all blessings to us; by whom we, being taught to live well, are sent on our way to life eternal.[11]

To accentuate this conviction, Clement blends the language of the New Testament with the language of philosophy. The message inherent in his literary method is that Jesus of Nazareth who healed the blind, who died to conquer death, is the same one who set the universe in order:

> He . . . who is the supramundane Wisdom, the celestial Word, is the all-harmonious, melodious, holy instrument of God. What, then, does this instrument—the Word of God, the Lord, the New Song—desire? To open the eyes of the blind, and unstop the ears of the deaf, and to lead the lame or the erring to righteousness, to exhibit God to the foolish, to put a stop to corruption, to conquer death, to reconcile disobedient children to their father. The instrument of God loves humankind.[12]

At the same time, Clement plays on the image of Orpheus, who tamed the wild beasts with his music. Christ is the *new* Orpheus, who, like David, does not teach idolatry or any of the other deceits of polytheistic myth, but rather liberates from the yoke of false worship:

> [The new song of Christ the Logos] has come to loose, . . . speedily, the bitter bondage of tyrannizing demons; and leading us back to the mild and loving yoke of piety, recalls to heaven those that had been cast prostrate to the earth.[13]

He polemicizes here against idolatry, the worship of "blocks of stone and wood—that is statues and paintings."[14] But he has tied this theme both literarily and philosophically to a broad range of religious issues. The "blocks of stone and wood" worshiped by the Gentiles bring to his mind the words of Jesus that "God is able from these stones to raise up children to Abraham" (Matt. 3:9; Luke 3:8).[15] The worshipers of idols, in the familiar words of the Psalmist, have "become like them"—ignorant and insensate. Likewise, the worshiper of false gods becomes beastlike and needs to be tamed by the new song of the Logos, which "alone has tamed people, the most intractable of animals" so that they, too, may become like what they worship, the Logos.[16]

Pursuing the musical metaphor, Clement observes that the transformative effect of the new song of the Logos on its listeners returns them to their true human nature. For we are "beautiful breathing instrument[s] of music" made "after [God's] own image" and "tuned by the Holy Spirit" along with the entire universe.[17] In their special role as the microcosm, consisting of body and soul, humans are addressed in song by God:

> "You are my harp, and pipe, and temple"—a harp for harmony—a pipe by reason of the Spirit—a temple by reason of the Word; so that the first may sound, the second breathe, the third contain the Lord.[18]

In these captivating images Clement has combined the Middle-Platonic Logos with allusions to the healing and reconciling ministry of Jesus of Nazareth and with a traditional biblical polemic against idolatry—all while co-opting the image of the soothing and ordering music of the pagan god Orpheus.[19]

The Savior as Sophia Incarnate

This Savior is not only the new Orpheus, he is also the new Sophia. For as Clement says:

> The Savior, who existed before, has in recent days appeared . . . as our Teacher . . . who now exhorts to salvation, as He has ever done, as He did by signs and wonders in Egypt and the desert, both by the bush and the cloud, which, through the favour of divine love, attended the Hebrews like a handmaid.[20]

Like Justin Martyr before him, Clement here identifies the Logos with the figure of Wisdom personified, and he sees this figure as the One who was present in the theophanies of Hebrew scripture. For him as for Justin, the figure of Wisdom, who exhorts us to follow her ways and to turn away from folly (Proverbs 8), is the same One who spoke through the prophets as well as to Moses in the burning bush. Neither of these second-century Christian writers invented these notions. Both Philo and the author of the Wisdom of Solomon attest a full development of a personified Wisdom or Logos figure who speaks and acts as the agent of God in the law and the prophets.[21] But the Christian writers take this identification one step further in seeing in the Word/Wisdom figure the same Savior who "has now appeared to human beings."[22]

When Clement adopts the Alexandrian Jewish Wisdom tradition and applies it to the man Jesus of Nazareth, he is faced with an anomaly. The personification of Sophia/Wisdom/Hokhmah had been elaborated along distinctly feminine lines.[23] She, the consort of God, may also become the bride of the sage, who says:

> Her I loved and sought out from my youth,
> and longed to make her my bride,
> and I became a lover of her beauty.
> She magnifies her noble birth by
> enjoying intimacy with God,
> and the Master of All loved her.
> For she is initiate in the knowledge of God,
> and chooser of his works.[24]

(Wisd. of Sol. 8:2–4)

Even the Alexandrian Jewish exegete and philosopher Philo, who dislikes female imagery for the Deity, preserves instances of such feminine metaphors, perhaps from earlier levels of Alexandrian exegetical tradition. When Justin adopted this sapiential material, he abandoned the distinctly female nuances. In an aside about the philosophical tradition allegorizing Athena's emergence from the head of Zeus as Wisdom emerging from the ineffable Deity, he reveals the basis of his choice: "They speak of Athena as the first thought; we regard it as ridiculous to propose the shape of females as the image of thought."[25]

Clement, by contrast, draws in these images of Wisdom as mother, giving predominance to the grammatically masculine Logos as the name of the Savior as well as to the sexually masculine incarnation of the Savior in Jesus, but he neither rejects nor ridicules the application of female metaphors to this preexistent divine being. Indeed, he transfers the imagery in startlingly graphic form to God the Father as well:

> To Christ the fulfilling of His Father's will was food; and to us infants, who milk the Word of the heavens, Christ Himself is food. Hence seeking is called sucking; for to those infants who seek the Word, the Father's nipples of the love of humankind supply milk.[26]

This image occurs in the context of Clement's proposal that we who may be accustomed to understand the eucharistic command to eat Christ's flesh and drink his blood not mystically but "perhaps more commonly" should now "hear it also in the following way." The flesh represents the Holy Spirit who created it; the blood represents the Logos. The union of both, "the Lord Jesus—that is, the Word of God, the Spirit made flesh," is both "the milk of the Father, by which . . . infants are suckled," and the "'care-soothing breast' [*Iliad* 22.83] of the Father." This milk is identical with the blood that Christ "shed . . . for us, to save humanity."[27] Indeed, he observes, "in many ways the Word is figuratively described [in scripture], as meat, and flesh, and food, and bread, and blood, and milk."[28] These are all compatible, since different physical and physiological conditions transform various liquids into solids and transform a mother's blood into milk for her infant.[29]

While we may become lost in Clement's metaphorical labyrinth, and we may even find his science somewhat dated, I think we cannot avoid being affected by his powerful maternal imagery and its theological import. In another passage he asserts:

> God, out of His great love of humankind, comes to the help of humankind, as the mother-bird flies to one of her young that has fallen out of the nest; and if a serpent open its mouth to swallow the little bird, "the mother flutters round, uttering cries of grief over her dear progeny" [*Iliad* 2.315]; and God the Father seeks His creature, and heals its transgression, and pursues the serpent, and recovers the young one, and incites it to fly up to the nest.[30]

These images of God as the nursing mother and as mother bird communicate with unique poignancy the depth of God's love of and commitment to human beings. The mother bird's rescue of her young contains another allegory important to Clement: She cannot simply rescue her little one but must urge it to imitate her and fly up to the nest.

The Savior as Teacher

Both these images of the Savior, as new Orpheus and as maternal Sophia, are closely related to the image of Christ the Teacher—first, the child's instructor in basic ethical behavior (the *paedagogos*), and second, the teacher of more advanced philosophical and spiritual doctrine (*didaskalos*). Clement uses these images to relate the varied biblical theologies to stages of ethical and spiritual development both for groups of people and for individuals.

First, within the Bible he portrays the Savior as the Christ-Orpheus who speaks or sings in a variety of tones, each suited to the addressee:

[The Savior], who from the beginning gave revelations by prophecy, but now plainly calls to salvation . . . has many tones of voice, and many methods for human salvation; by threatening He admonishes, by reproaching He converts, by bewailing He pities, by the voice of song He cheers.[31]

Second, having recognized the multiple tones of the Savior testified in the Bible, Clement was willing to allow that the same Savior had spoken through certain Greek philosophers and some barbarian sages, as we have already noted. He also implicitly recognized that the Savior spoke to and through the ancient Greek literary tradition—Homer and Hesiod, the tragedians, and the poets in general. Thus his work is punctuated with allusions to ancient Greek literature that are meant not merely to establish him as a man of wide learning but, more important, to show that to the discerning scholar the entire history of humanity bears witness to the loving communication of the Savior. Often even without the understanding of the poet, the Savior has spoken the words of truth to humankind, always in the tones appropriate to their state of religious awareness and their level of ethical advancement.

Yet this is the one and the same God who has spoken to all human beings in every time, place, and culture. Further, the message, most clearly and fully set forth in the incarnation, is always fundamentally the same: God loves and cares for humankind and calls us to become Godlike. For, he says, "now the Word Himself clearly converses with you, shaming your unbelief. Yes, I say, the Word of God became human that you may learn from a human being how a human being may become God."[32]

How is this transformation to be achieved? Clement's *paedagogos* provides the first level of instruction. Here he addresses a multifarious array of topics pertaining to proper behavior. He offers advice on eating, drinking, bathing, exercise, sexual behavior, and appropriate styles of walking, as well as on home furnishings, clothing, jewelry, makeup, and whether or not to pluck the hair, especially the beard. The specificity and comprehensiveness of his admonitions provide a treasure trove of the mores and trappings of aristocratic life in the Roman Empire, not to speak of a welcome note of levity for the diligent student of the Church Fathers. He counsels, for example, that at banquets one ought to avoid whistling, blowing the nose, coughing, spitting, belching, sneezing, and scratching the ears.[33] As to elegant footwear, white sandals should suffice; the "foolish artistries of golden and gem-studded sandals, of Attic and Sicyonian boots, and buskins, and Persian and Tyrrhenian slippers as well" are to be given up.[34] In this day of designer sheets and elaborate bedding, we might be well advised to update and heed his advice to eschew gold embroidery, purple dyes, silver-footed couches, and downy feathers because, after all, "Jacob slept on the ground with a stone for his pillow."[35]

The point of all this is that we seek true beauty, which consists in the adornment not of the body but of the soul. To that end we must pursue self-control, self-sufficiency, and moderation of the passions.[36] Clement's audience, clearly presumed to be aristocratic, male and female, is advised not to be overly dependent on slaves. They, too, are created in the image of God; but more important, lack of self-sufficiency would stand in the way of moral progress.[37] In his advice and its rationale he simply reaffirms Stoic ethical teaching, as was well known in his time, as it is in ours.

But we must also remember that the ultimate goal of Christian life is not the moderation of the passions but their extirpation and the subsequent stage of assimilation to God, the more purely Platonic phase of Clement's ethic. This is the subject of the *Stromateis*. All are called to this stage—slave and free, male and female are meant to become philosophers and "knowing witnesses" to Christ, who now takes the role of *didaskalos,* the teacher of higher philosophical and spiritual doctrines.

Clement has been appreciated for his emphasis on the equal summoning of women to "philosophize," that is, to respond to the same call to virtue, based on their possession of the same nature as men's, and on their full possession of the *imago dei* ("image of God").[38] He reinforces the point with a catalogue of women drawn from the Bible and from Greek philosophical traditions. These women, commemorated for their pursuit of the higher level of perfection through heroic self-denial, include Judith, Esther, Susanna, and Miriam (who, however, is identified only as "the sister of Moses"). Also mentioned is Lysidica, who "through excess of modesty, bathed in her clothes" and Theano the Pythagorean, who made "such progress in philosophy, that to him who looked intently at her, and said, 'Your arm is beautiful,' she answered 'Yes, but it is not public.'"[39]

In the midst of these anecdotes, we must be reminded of the seriousness of our calling to likeness to God. On the other hand, to post-Freudian ears the extirpation of the passions sounds like repression of feelings. Without making unrealistic and anachronistic claims for Clement and his monastic heirs, we should note that the passions—which include prominently not only sexual desire but also anger—are first to be gradually moderated as one moves toward the goal of *apatheia*. This is closer to sublimation than to repression. In his discussion of the Beatitudes, moreover, Clement relates the extirpation of anger to the command to love our enemies, thus reminding us also that the love of humankind is not one of the passions.[40] It is the characteristic attitude of the one Savior who lovingly summons us all in varied tones to become ever more Godlike—thus more philanthropic.

Conclusion

Christians in the first centuries used female metaphors, and especially the image of Sophia, the Wisdom of God, in theological and devotional contexts.[41] Clement of Alexandria provides an example of the use of female theological metaphor from this formative period of Christian theology and piety. I have couched the presentation of his dramatic imagery in a fuller discussion of his understanding of theology in relation to culture. I have argued that Clement reflects self-consciously and honestly on his process of selection. Although he adopts ideas, phrases, and even entire blocks of material from Greek literary tradition, from Middle-Platonic philosophy, from Alexandrian Judaism, and from earlier Christian interpreters, including even some he himself deems heretical, he has thought carefully about how to fit them together and which notions are to be excluded. Nonetheless, his Christian vision is presented in rich imagery and with a joyful spirit of inclusiveness. His readiness to use feminine metaphors for the divine saving love is a dimension of his versatile and imaginative appropriation of Greek literature and religious lore alongside the biblical heritage.

Although he would probably question some aspects of the Re-imagining Conference, Clement surely shares some of its spirit. His communion of spirit with feminist theologians is not limited to his readiness to use female theological language. It is also found in his profound appreciation of the beauty and goodness of the creation and in his insistence on the universal human calling to grow constantly into the divine likeness. None of these features of Clement's theology prevents his being relentlessly Christocentric. He is utterly convinced that the fullness of truth rests not only in scripture but in scripture read through the lens of the incarnation. Yet this does not prevent his deep conviction that the Savior who appeared in these last days in human form has been using every human religion and every little bit of truth in philosophy to call out, indeed to sing, to humankind, to lure us as little fishes with his bait, to feed us at his breast

Kathleen E. McVey

with the milk of wisdom, and to draw us into his loving embrace so that we may be Christ-begotten co-citizens with God.

Notes

A portion of this chapter appeared under the title "Christianity and Culture, Dead White European Males, and the Study of Patristics" in *The Princeton Seminary Bulletin*, n.s., 15 (1994): 103–30. Fuller documentation and discussion may be found there.

1. For a brief survey, see Ritamary Bradley, "Patristic Background of the Motherhood Similitude in Julian of Norwich," *Christian Scholar's Review* 8 (1978):101–13.
2. For English translations, see William Wilson, trans., "Exhortation to the Heathen," "The Instructor," and "The Stromata, or Miscellanies," in *Fathers of the Second Century,* The Ante-Nicene Fathers 2 (Grand Rapids: Wm. B. Eerdmans, 1951), 171–568; Simon P. Wood, trans., *Clement of Alexandria: Christ the Educator,* The Fathers of the Church 23 (New York: Fathers of the Church, 1954); and John Ferguson, trans., *Clement of Alexandria: Stromateis: Books One to Three,* The Fathers of the Church 85 (Washington, D.C.: Catholic University of America Press, 1991).
3. *Strom.* 1.11.50–51; cf. 1 Cor. 3:19–21. Trans. Ferguson, *Stromateis,* 59–60.
4. *Strom.* 1.11.52.3. My translation.
5. W. E. G. Floyd, *Clement of Alexandria's Treatment of the Problem of Evil,* Oxford Theological Monographs (London: Oxford University Press, 1971), esp. 35–40.
6. See Floyd, *Clement,* 3–5; and Salvatore R. C. Lilla, *Clement of Alexandria: A Study in Christian Platonism and Gnosticism,* Oxford Theological Monographs (London: Oxford University Press, 1971), 193–99.
7. Lilla, *Clement of Alexandria,* esp. 87, 94, 104, 106–7; Raoul Mortley, *Connaissance Religieuse et Herméneutique chez Clément d'Alexandrie* (Leiden: E. J. Brill, 1973), esp. 156.
8. Lilla, *Clement of Alexandria,* 60–117; Mortley, *Connaissance Religieuse et Herméneutique,* 109–57.
9. *Protrept.* 1.4.5. Trans. Wilson, "Exhortation," 172 (modified).
10. *Protrept.* 1.6.1, 1.6.5, 1.7.3. Thomas Halton, "Clement's Lyre: A Broken String, A New Song," *The Second Century* 3 (1983):177–99.
11. *Protrept.* 1.7.1. Trans. Wilson, "Exhortation," 173 (modified).
12. *Protrept.* 1.5.4–1.6.2. Trans. Wilson, "Exhortation," 172 (modified).
13. *Protrept.* 1.3.2. Trans. Wilson, "Exhortation," 172.
14. *Protrept.* 1.3.1. Trans. Wilson, "Exhortation," 172 (modified).
15. *Protrept.* 1.4.2. Trans. Wilson, "Exhortation," 172.
16. *Protrept.* 1.4.1. Trans. Wilson, "Exhortation," 172 (modified).
17. *Protrept.* 1.5.4, 1.5.3. Trans. Wilson, "Exhortation," 172.
18. *Protrept.* 1.5.3. Trans. Wilson, "Exhortation," 172 (modified).
19. The polemic against anthropomorphic polytheism is, of course, also philo-

sophical; see Paul Corby Finney, *The Invisible God: The Earliest Christians on Art* (New York: Oxford University Press, 1994).

20. *Protrept.* 1.7.3, 1.8.1. Trans. Wilson, "Exhortation," 173.
21. David Winston, *The Wisdom of Solomon: A New Translation with Introduction and Commentary,* The Anchor Bible 43 (New York: Doubleday, 1979), esp. 33–62. For Philo, see Burton L. Mack, *Logos und Sophia: Untersuchungen zur Weisheitstheologie im hellenistischen Judentum,* Studien zur Umwelt des Neuen Testaments 10 (Göttingen: Vandenhoeck & Ruprecht, 1973).
22. *Protrept.* 1.7.1.
23. For a survey of the materials and issues, see Joan C. Engelsman, *The Feminine Dimension of the Divine* (Philadelphia: Westminster Press, 1979).
24. Trans. Winston, *Wisdom,* 191. Cf. Wisdom of Solomon 8:16 and Winston's discussion, *Wisdom,* 192–96.
25. Justin *First Apology* 64.5 (Edgar J. Goodspeed, ed., *Die älteste Apologeten* [Göttingen: Vandenhoeck & Ruprecht, 1984], 73–74).
26. *Paed.* 1.6.46.1. Trans. Wilson, "Instructor," 221 (modified).
27. *Paed.* 1.6.43.2–4 passim. Trans. Wilson, "Instructor," 220 (modified).
28. *Paed.* 1.6.47.2 passim. Trans. Wilson, "Instructor," 221.
29. *Paed.* 1.6.44.1–45.3; cf. 1.6.39–41.
30. *Protrept.* 10.91.3. Trans. Wilson, "Exhortation," 197 (modified).
31. *Protrept.* 1.7.6–8.3. Trans. Wilson, "Exhortation," 173 (modified).
32. *Protrept.* 1.8.4. Trans. Wilson, "Exhortation," 174 (modified).
33. *Paed.* 2.7.60.
34. *Paed.* 2.11.116.2–117.1. Trans. Wood, *Christ the Educator,* 189.
35. *Paed.* 2.9.77–78. Trans. Wood, *Christ the Educator,* 159–60.
36. *Paed.* 1.12.98.4, 3.2.4.1, 3.6.35.3, 3.7.38.3.
37. *Strom.* 4.8.58–69; and see n. 36.
38. *Strom.* 4.8.58–69. See Kari Elisabeth Børresen, "God's Image, Man's Image? Patristic Interpretation of Gen. 1, 27 and I Cor. 11, 7," in *Image of God and Gender Models in Judaeo-Christian Tradition,* ed. Kari E. Børresen (Oslo: Solum Forlag, 1991), 188–207, esp. 194–96. But see also Donald Kinder, "Clement of Alexandria: Conflicting Views on Women," *The Second Century* 7 (1989–90): 213–20.
39. *Strom.* 4.19.118.1–123.1, esp. 119.1–3, 120.1, 121.2. Trans. Wilson, "Stromata," 431.
40. *Strom.* 4.14.95–96.
41. There has yet to be a comprehensive discussion of this usage and its relation to the development of doctrines in the early church. In a forthcoming work, I hope to take up this larger matter.

5

Lover and Mother:
Medieval Language for God and the Soul

F ather, Mother, Bridegroom, and Lover. The current quest to appropriate the wealth of biblical images for God, especially for Christ, may seem creative and even daring in its "re-imagining," but not in comparison to the verbal versatility of certain medieval authors, women and men. On this point, writers from the Middle Ages may surprise us. Their agility in speaking about God and the soul in both masculine and feminine terms, sometimes in the same sentence, can instruct us about the diversity and flexibility of the Christian tradition over the centuries.

The authors surveyed here were steeped in scriptural language, day and night, in corporate worship and individual meditation. Their creative, sometimes poetic, expressions were grounded in biblical precedents. These women and men were familiar with the multifaceted relationship of gender and language. In Latin, as in the original biblical languages, a noun like *wisdom* or *church* could have a gender that was unrelated to its meaning, simply an irrelevant accident of nomenclature. But the Bible's own imagery sometimes went beyond grammatical gender to personify some such terms, as in "Wisdom" as a woman (Proverbs 9) or the church as "the bride of Christ." These and other personifications were emphasized still further in the spiritual exegesis of the Middle Ages, especially in the language of marriage and motherhood.

These medieval authors were not speaking about God or Christ in the abstract, in some detached isolation from themselves. They were ardently expressing an intimate relatedness to God, which meant a parallel creativity in language for their own side of this loving relationship.[1] The language of lovers and mothers was used both for God and also for one's own soul, sometimes with striking agility, disregarding the author's biological gender and switching metaphors in midsentence.

The Language of Lovers

Both the Old and New Testaments provided medieval authors with a solid foundation for speaking about the divine-human relationship in the language of lovers. Husband and wife, bridegroom and bride were common human images for the commitment and love of God for Israel and the church. The book of Hosea provided extended warrant, and Ephesians 5:22 as combined with Revelation 21:2 supplied the image of the church as the bride of Christ, the heavenly husband.

The fullest presentation of this motif was the Song of Solomon, emphasized in the Middle Ages as much as it is neglected today: "My beloved is mine and I am his" (2:16). This love song was first applied corporately to God and Israel and then, by Christian exegetes, to Christ and the church. Ardor alternates with despair as the lover seeks out her beloved: "I sought him whom my soul loves; I sought him, but found him not" (3:1). Early Christian interpretation of the Song of Solomon understood the beloved as Christ: "My beloved is all radiant and ruddy. . . . His speech is most sweet, and he is altogether desirable" (5:10a, 16a). In the third century Origen of Alexandria added to the Bible's imagery of the bride as the corporate Israel or the church an emphasis on the individual dimension, namely, the bride as one's soul.

> For whether she is the soul made after His image or the Church, she has fallen deeply in love with Him. Moreover, this book of scripture instructs us in the words this marvelous and perfect bridegroom uses toward the soul or the Church that has been united with him.[2]

Origen's interpretation of the bride/lover and bridegroom/beloved as the soul and Christ was elaborated on at length by many medieval authors, especially Bernard of Clairvaux, the immensely influential twelfth-century abbot. Bernard wrote dozens of sermons on the Song of Solomon, saying, for instance, "The word of God himself, the soul's bridegroom, comes to the soul as he wishes."[3] Bernard's devotion to Christ's body, borrowed from the Song of Solomon's references to the beloved's head and arms and legs, added a focus on Christ crucified and lives on in hymns such as "Wide Open Are Your Hands" and "O Sacred Head, Now Wounded." And who is the soul who longs for this beloved? About this, Bernard is emphatic: "I will unhesitatingly attribute to her the voice and name of bride, and I shall consider everything this passage says to be applicable to her."[4] Later in the same sermon, Bernard provides a rare glimpse into his own spiritual experience, making explicit what has been implied throughout, that Christ relates as male bridegroom to one's own soul as female bride, whatever one's biological gender. "And so when the bridegroom, the Word, came to me, he never made any sign that he was coming. Only by the warmth of my heart did I know he was there."[5] Note that Bernard speaks plainly of Christ as male, and himself, a male author, as the female bride. His biological gender did not limit his creative appropriation of the biblical imagery.

There are many other examples of "bridal mysticism" in the Middle

Ages, especially among women authors. As early as the martyrdom of Perpetua (c. 200), a specific woman is called "spouse of Christ."[6] Among the many medieval "Brides of the Celestial Bedchamber" are Beatrice of Nazareth (Belgium, 1200–1268) and Mechthild of Magdeburg.[7] At the climax of Beatrice's *Seven Manners of Holy Love* she exults: "There will the soul become one with her Bridegroom and become one spirit with him in a troth that can never be parted, in everlasting Minne [Love]."[8] Mechthild of Magdeburg (1210–1280) wrote about love in many poetic ways, including a continuation of Bernard's exegesis of the Song of Solomon: "Our Redeemer has become our bridegroom! The bride has become drunk at the sight of his noble face."[9] She also adds the dimension of poetic chivalry. "When the poor soul comes to Court, she is prudent and well-behaved. She joyfully gazes at her God. Then she says 'Lord, you art my solace, my desire, my flowing stream.'"[10] Not only does Mechthild here add a note of chivalry or courtly love as did many medieval poets; she also juxtaposes the language of lovers with other ways of speaking about God, even in the same sentence: "I must to [go] God—//My Father through nature, //My Brother through humanity,//My Bridegroom through love, //His am I for ever!"[11] Here, again, we see a remarkable dexterity in the rapid change of language for God, from Father in creation, to Brother in incarnation, to Bridegroom in loving union.

The nuptial imagery for Christ and the soul was widespread in the Middle Ages, with frequent attention to the body of Christ as the loving bridegroom. Hadewijch of Antwerp (thirteenth century) goes even further with the human metaphor of marital relations. In one of her many visions she recounts:

> With that he came in the form and clothing of a Man . . . wonderful, and beautiful, and with a glorious face . . . he came himself to me, took me entirely in his arms, and pressed me to him; and all my members felt his in full felicity, in accordance with the desires of my heart and my humanity. So I was outwardly satisfied and fully transported.[12]

Hadewijch may be describing a spiritual experience that had a physiological component as well, or perhaps this is simply a daring literary extension of the language of lovers. In any case, Hadewijch provides us with another example of the verbal versatility of medieval authors regarding gender references for God and the soul.

So far, these examples have retained the biblical model of Christ as the male bridegroom and the soul as female. But Hadewijch's adaptation of the courtly literature of "Minne" or "Lady Love" also inverts the image. In the idiom of the medieval troubadours, Hadewijch personifies Love as Lady Love, leaving the Soul who woos and is wounded by love to be male:

> Love conquers him so that he may conquer her; . . .
> When he experiences this sweet Love,

He is wounded with her wounds; . . .
He imbibes eagerly from Love's deep veins,
With continual thirst for a new beginning,
Until he enjoys sweet Love.[13]

Here Hadewijch draws more from medieval love poetry than the biblical Song of Solomon. But notice her own flexibility. As Bernard could identify himself with the female image for the soul, so Hadewijch identifies herself with male imagery. An author's own gender could be transcended by his or her creative inspiration regarding gendered language for God and the soul.

The Language of Mothers

The language of motherhood was prominent among medieval authors, not only for Jesus as Mother but also for the soul. Several women of the Middle Ages had visions of Jesus as a baby, sometimes identifying themselves as the affectionate and occasionally nursing mother. Marie d'Oignies (1177–1213) told her biographer:

Sometimes it seemed to her that for three or more days she held Him close to her so that He nestled between her breasts like a baby, and she hid Him there lest He be seen by others.[14]

Similarly, Gertrude the Great (1256–1302) had a Christmas Eve vision in which she assisted the Virgin and then herself experienced the intimate maternal bond:

In this night, I say, my Soul beheld before it suddenly a delicate Child, but just born, in whom were concealed the greatest gifts of perfection. I imagined that I received this precious deposit in my bosom with the tenderest affection.[15]

Such gendered references to the soul as mother with reference to Jesus as a baby are not rare,[16] but they are far outnumbered by the wide array of references to Jesus himself as mother. Here the biblical background is not the nativity scene but several scattered verses. In Isaiah, God is likened to the compassionate mother: "Can a woman forget her nursing child, or show no compassion for the child of her womb? Even these may forget, yet I will not forget you" (Isa. 49:15). The feminine image of Wisdom is also part of the story, and Jesus himself compared God to a woman seeking a lost coin (Luke 15:8–10). But most influential is Jesus' self-description in maternal terms, "as a hen gathers her brood under her wings" (Matt. 23:37).[17]

The medieval adaptations of this biblical imagery of motherhood regarding God were frequent, but not what many modern readers expect.

The title of "mother" was not usually applied to the first person of the Trinity as an alternative to "father" language, but rather to the second person, as a way of speaking about Christ. There are only a few scattered instances of maternal imagery attached to the paternal for the first person of the Godhead. The Abbess Hildegard of Bingen (twelfth century) spoke of "the embrace of God's maternal love."[18] Hadewijch juxtaposed female and male references: "love dwells so deep in the womb of the Father."[19] Although unusual, such expressions were not unprecedented; the Council of Toledo in 675 had spoken of the Son coming "from the womb of the Father."[20] These rare examples are dwarfed by the substantial tradition throughout the Middle Ages in which male and female authors alike used maternal images to characterize Christ.[21] After the precedents of the early church, the medieval pattern is set by St. Anselm, Archbishop of Canterbury in the eleventh century and prominent medieval theologian:

> And you, Jesus, are you not also a mother?
>   Are you not the mother who, like a hen,
>   gathers her chickens under her wings?
> Truly, Lord, you are a mother;
>   for both they who are in labour
>   and they who are brought forth
>   are accepted by you.
> You have died more than they, that they may labour to bear.
>   It is by your death that they have been born,
>   for if you had not been in labour
>   you could not have borne death;
> and if you had not died, you would not have brought forth.
>   For, longing to bear sons into life,
>   you tasted of death,
>   and by dying you begot them.
> You did this in your own self,
>   your servants by your commands and help.
>   You as the author, they as the ministers.
>   So you, Lord God, are the great mother.[22]

After Anselm, there were more detailed descriptions of Jesus' death in terms of labor pains in giving birth. These images built on Isaiah 42:14: "For a long time I have held my peace,//I have kept still and restrained myself;//now I will cry out like a woman in labor,//I will gasp and pant." Marguerite D'Oingt (1240–1310), prioress of a Carthusian convent near Lyons, gave up her mother and father but said of Christ:

> For are you not my mother and more than my mother? The mother who bore me labored in delivering me for one day or one night but you, my sweet and lovely Lord, labored for me for more than thirty years. Ah . . . with what love you labored for me and bore me through your whole life. But when the time approached for you to be delivered, your labor pains

were so great that your holy sweat was like great drops of blood that came
out from your body and fell on the earth. . . . Ah! Sweet Lord Jesus Christ,
who ever saw a mother suffer such a birth! For when the hour of your de-
livery came you were placed on the hard bed of the cross . . . and your
nerves and all your veins were broken. And truly it is no surprise that your
veins burst when in one day you gave birth to the whole world.[23]

St. Bernard was the most thorough of twelfth-century authors on this
point. Following the lead of Anselm, he used mother language to describe
Jesus, Moses, Peter, Paul, church leaders in general, abbots in particular,
and himself most particularly. His emphasis was not on conceiving and
giving birth, but on nursing and breast feeding. This image to him represented generous love for others:

> If you feel the stings of temptation . . . suck not so much the wounds as
> the breasts of the Crucified. He will be your mother and you will be his
> son.[24]

For Bernard, the image of breasts in the Song of Solomon is not the sexuality language of the male bridegroom to the female bride, but that of the
soul seeking out the nourishment of Christ: "Your breasts are better than
wine" (1:2; Vulg.). Bernard often referred to Christ as a nursing mother
feeding us from himself as from breasts and the blood from his side. His
contemporary William of St. Thierry also interpreted the Song of Solomon
this way: "it is your breasts, O eternal Wisdom, that nourish the holy in-
fancy of your little ones."[25] The Incarnation itself was understood in this
mode of accommodating nourishment: "It was not the least of the chief
reasons for your incarnation that your babes in the church, who still
needed your milk rather than solid food, who are not strong enough
spiritually to think of you in your own way, might find in you a form not
unfamiliar to themselves."[26]

Still more authors of the Middle Ages used female and especially maternal images for Christ:

> The Bridegroom . . . has breasts, lest he should be lacking any one of
> all duties and titles of loving kindness. He is a father in virtue of natural
> creation . . . and also in virtue of the authority with which he instructs.
> He is a mother, too, in the mildness of his affection, and a nurse.[27]

Elisabeth of Schönau, a twelfth-century Benedictine visionary, also had
special revelations, including a vision of a bright sun and the likeness of
a woman in its midst:

> On the holy day of Christmas, now, when the solemnities were being
> celebrated, I asked the holy angel of God who appeared to me, what
> sort of vision it was and what significance it had. He replied to me con-
> cerning that Virgin, for I especially desired to know who she was. He
> said "that virgin whom you see, is the sacred humanity of the Lord Jesus.

The sun on which the virgin is enthroned is the Godhead which wholly contains and illuminates the humanity of the Savior.[28]

And, of course, there are the justly famous descriptions of Jesus as mother in the writings of the anchoress, Julian of Norwich (1343–1413):

> The mother can give her child to suck of her milk, but our precious Mother Jesus can feed us with himself, and does, most courteously and most tenderly, with the blessed sacrament which is the precious food of true life.[29]

This imagery is treated at length in Julian and was well known to her contemporaries and to posterity. Breast milk was frequently associated with Christ's blood and sacramental wine.

> The mother can lay her child tenderly to her breast, but our tender Mother Jesus can lead us easily into his blessed breast through his sweet open side, and show us there a part of the godhead and of the joys of heaven, with inner certainty of endless bliss. . . .
>
> This fair lovely word "mother" is so sweet and so kind in itself that it cannot truly be said of anyone or to anyone except of him and to him who is the true Mother of life and of all things. To the property of motherhood belong nature, love, wisdom, and knowledge, and this is God.[30]

Conclusion

Julian of Norwich also represents the flexibility of language that has been illustrated throughout this chapter. She is able to use both the language of mother and also the language of lovers:

> And so in our making, God Almighty is our loving Father, and God all wisdom is our loving Mother, with the love and the goodness of the Holy Spirit, which is all one God, one Lord. And in the joining and the union he is our very true spouse and we his beloved wife and his fair maiden, with which wife he was never displeased; for he says: I love you and you love me, and our love will never divide in two.[31]

As Julian quickly added to the language of mother the language of lover, many medieval authors can surprise us with their capacity for holding multiple scriptural images together. In a vision of Mechthild of Hackeborn (1240–1298), Christ sends a message of comfort to a discouraged sister:

> I am her father by creation, her mother by redemption, her brother in the sharing of my kingdom, her sister by dear companionship.[32]

This creativity was often honored and welcomed in the church of that time, for two reasons. First, such authors were usually considered to be visionaries or spiritual authorities who enjoyed a certain poetic license in their works. None of the writers surveyed here was prosecuted for theological heresy. Many of them are accepted by Christian tradition as saints, and several, such as Anselm and Bernard, are among the favorite authorities of Roman Catholics and Protestants alike. Second, even when ecclesiastical authorities were suspicious of certain women mystics, their descriptions using the biblical language of motherhood were carefully confined to the second person of the Godhead within an orthodox theology of the Trinity. Furthermore, Jesus as mother was always male in pronoun.

In general, this wide range of images can provoke diverse reactions. Self-styled traditionalists may be challenged by the deep reservoirs of Christian tradition regarding creative uses of the language of lovers and mothers for God. The more graphic, bodily images of breast feeding and sexual relations may offend some modern sensibilities. Those eager for such creativity, on the other hand, may be challenged by the heavy emphasis on the maleness of Christ in the imagery of lover, and by the tendency to restrict mother language to Christology instead of to a general doctrine of God. Although few modern readers will find all of the images presented here to be equally congenial, our very discomfort with one or more of these daring applications of biblical imagery is testimony to the bold creativity of medieval authors.

Notes

1. The best general introduction to the history of Christian spirituality is Bernard McGinn's multivolumed work currently in progress. *The Presence of God: A History of Western Christian Mysticism,* vol. 1, *The Foundations of Mysticism: Origins to the Fifth Century;* and vol. 2, *The Growth of Mysticism: Gregory the Great Through the 12th Century* (New York: Crossroad, 1992 and 1994).
2. Origen, *Exhortation to Martyrdom and Other Works,* trans. Rowan Green (New York: Paulist Press, 1979), 217.
3. *Bernard of Clairvaux: Selected Works,* trans. G. R. Evans (New York: Paulist Press, 1987), 253.
4. Ibid.
5. Ibid., 255.
6. "The Martyrdom of Perpetua," in *The Acts of Christian Martyrs,* ed. H. Musurillo (Oxford: Clarendon Press, 1972), 126–27.
7. The phrase is from Marcelle Thiébaux, trans., *The Writings of Medieval Women,* 2d ed. (New York: Garland, 1994), 385. Hereafter cited as Thiébaux.
8. From "The Seventh Minne" of *The Seven Manners of Holy Minne* in Thiébaux, 410.
9. *The Flowing Light of the Godhead,* bk. I, chap. 22, in Thiébaux, 399.
10. Ibid., bk. I, chap. 4, in Thiébaux, 397. See also Elizabeth A. Petroff, ed., *Medieval Women's Visionary Literature* (New York: Oxford University Press, 1986), 215. Hereafter cited as Petroff.

11. Petroff, 220.
12. Vision 7 in *Hadewijch: The Complete Works,* trans. Columba Hart (New York: Paulist Press, 1980), 281 (hereafter cited as *Hadewijch*); also in Petroff, 196.
13. Stanzaic Poem 40 in *Hadewijch,* 244.
14. *Life of Marie,* bk. II, chap. 88, in Petroff, 182.
15. Petroff, 10.
16. See also *Margaret Ebner, Major Works,* trans. Leonard P. Hindsley (New York: Paulist Press, 1993).
17. On wisdom, see chapters 3 and 4 in this volume.
18. Hildegard of Bingen, *Scivias* II, 2, 4, trans. Mother Columba Hart and Jane Bishop (New York: Paulist Press, 1990), 162. In the 1911 translation cited by Petroff (p. 153), the word "maternal" was translated as "paternal."
19. Stanzaic Poem 8, trans. Ria Vanderauwera, in *Medieval Women Writers,* ed. Katherina Wilson (Athens: University of Georgia Press, 1984), 198.
20. Council of Toledo, "de Patris utero," in *Enchiridion Symbolorum,* ed. H. Denzinger, 32d ed. (Rome: Herder, 1963), 176.
21. See esp. Caroline Bynum's essay "Jesus as Mother and Abbot as Mother," in *Jesus as Mother: Studies in the Spirituality of the High Middle Ages* (Berkeley: University of California Press, 1982), 110–69. Hereafter cited as Bynum.
22. *The Prayers and Meditations of Saint Anselm,* trans. Benedicta Ward (Harmondsworth, Eng.: Penguin Books, 1973), 153–54.
23. Marguerite, in Bynum, 153, also cited in Petroff, 279.
24. Letter 322, in Bynum, 117.
25. William of St. Thierry, in Bynum, 119.
26. Bynum, 119–20.
27. Ibid., 122, quoting Guerric of Igny (d. 1157).
28. Thiébaux, 362.
29. Julian of Norwich, *Showings* (New York: Paulist Press, 1978), long text, chap. 60, 298.
30. Ibid, 298–99.
31. Ibid., long text, chap. 58, 293.
32. Mechthild of Hackeborn, *Livre* 4.50.296; in Mary J. Finnegan, *The Women of Helfta: Scholars and Mystics* (Athens: University of Georgia Press, 1991), 37–38.

6

Hearing a Different Message: Reforming Women Interpret the Bible

S elf-conscious attempts by women to read the Bible in the context of their own experience as women are not peculiar to the late twentieth century. At least as long ago as the late fourteenth and early fifteenth centuries, a few reforming women believed that wrong reading of the Bible was at the root of injustice to women. These women heard a different message about women in the Bible than the clergy did. Although the clergy declared that women were daughters of Eve, weaker than men but given to seducing men into sin, these women paid attention to the presence of women in the biblical texts and realized that many were strong and courageous. Whereas the clergy emphasized biblical passages that teach women's subordination, the women urged the reading of a broader range of biblical texts, including those that would demonstrate women's partnership in God's work.

To offer examples of some of the reforming messages these women heard in the Bible, I will turn to the writings of four reforming women. The first three are connected in various ways to French humanism over two centuries: Christine de Pisan (or de Pizan), a Catholic woman writing in the late fourteenth and early fifteenth centuries in France; Marguerite, Queen of Navarre, a Catholic woman in the sixteenth century with strong sympathies for humanist reform movements in her church; and Marie Dentière, a Catholic nun and abbess of her convent, who became a Protestant missionary to Geneva in the sixteenth century.[1] From a different context comes a German Lutheran woman of the sixteenth century, Argula von Grumbach, a noblewoman from Bavaria.

Unlike the medieval women writers discussed by Paul Rorem in chapter 5, these were laywomen, married women with children. Though they had considerable education of varied sorts and acquaintance with theology and the Bible, none had a university education or formal theological education, and most did not read Greek or Hebrew. The same could be said about the education of most of the Catholic parish clergy during this time period, however. All of these women were involved in some way in the public arena, in addition to managing their households. They came to their reading of the Bible with fresh eyes and different questions than did the clergy.

The Humanist Debate About Women

A significant intellectual debate about the nature of women flourished in humanist circles, mostly in France and England, from the very late fourteenth till about the seventeenth century, beginning with Christine de Pisan.[2] Women and men argued whether the weaknesses apparent in women should be attributed to their womanly nature itself or to the inferior education and restricted lives that shaped their experience. In other words, is women's apparent inferiority to men a problem of nature or of nurture? Obviously, one of the critical authorities for this debate was the Bible, as it was variously understood.

We should be clear that the debate did not divide neatly according to gender lines. A few of the men supported women, arguing that women's faults are the result of their socialization and are not inherent in female nature. In fact, the soaring rhetoric in some of the male defenses of women reminds us that in this debate one must allow for the element of sarcasm and hyperbole on both sides.

We should also be clear that the number of women from the Renaissance and Reformation periods who were sufficiently educated to have left us written evidence of their views of the message of scripture is small indeed. Scholars continue to locate, identify, and publish texts of women's religious writings from this period, so the number of sources available for research is growing. However, we dare not generalize from these authors to other women of the period, about whose views we know very little. Nor can we rely uncritically on what male writers of the time tell us about women's thinking. The men may or may not have been good listeners.

Let us turn to our four reforming women to explore their ways of reading the Bible and to see what sort of untraditional messages they heard there.

Christine de Pisan

Born in Italy, the daughter of a Renaissance professor at the University of Bologna, Christine was taken as a small child to France where her father had an appointment at the royal court. She grew up better educated than most women, but she still regretted that she had not been given the formal education available to men. When her husband's early death left her responsible for support of her family without adequate resources, she became a professional writer, a rare accomplishment for a woman of the time. Deeply offended by the misogyny of the *Roman de la Rose,* a popular example of the literature of courtly love, in 1399 she wrote a poem in protest that set off the literary debate about the nature of women. Christine's works were widely disseminated and often translated, extending her influence across Europe for centuries.[3]

Among Christine's many writings, one titled *The Book of the City of Ladies* (1405) illustrates our topic particularly well. She begins by telling of her disgust with so many books which claim that "the behaviour of women is inclined to and full of every vice."[4] She reflects on her own experience and that of women she knows and does not see the resemblance to the picture drawn by the male writers, some of whom are clergy. But she comes to the conclusion that the learned male scholars must be right, and she relies on their judgment more than her own personal knowledge. This leads her to despise herself and all women; she raises a despairing lament to God over God's creation of woman as such a vile creature, lacking the perfection men are said to have.[5]

Three crowned ladies suddenly appear to Christine and identify themselves as Reason, Rectitude, and Justice. Under their tutelage she learns that she is called to build with their help a city for virtuous women as a refuge, now that "it is time for their just cause to be taken from Pharaoh's hands."[6] She is taught to clear away the rubble for the foundation with the pick of understanding by asking questions of Reason; and she learns to use critical judgment toward male intellectual authorities, recognizing their denunciations of women as evil to be lies and ignorance. She learns to distinguish truth from falsehood and to have confidence in her own judgment. She is led back to the biblical story of the creation of woman in the image of God as a noble creature with a soul equally as good as that of man.[7]

Christine is also instructed from the Gospels to understand that Jesus Christ did not despise women. Typical traits of women that are attacked by men, causing Christine great pain, are shown to be respected by Jesus. The charge that "women by nature have a servile heart and that they are like infants" is countered by Jesus' placing the child before the quarreling apostles: "I tell you that whoever humbles himself like this child shall be the most rewarded." The attacks on women's natural tendency to talk and weep are countered by the stories of Jesus' compassion for the weeping of Mary and Martha at the death of Lazarus, followed by his resurrection of Lazarus. He accepted the tears of Mary Magdalene and forgave her sins. He was moved by the tears of the widow and brought her dead son back to life. God endowed women with speech, and the Lord Jesus Christ commanded Mary Magdalene, to whom he appeared after his resurrection, to announce the news to the apostles. Furthermore, the Canaanite woman was a great talker who just kept crying after Jesus, and he rewarded her great faith.

Who could sufficiently sum up this honor paid to the feminine sex which the jealous despise, considering that in the heart of this little bit of a pagan woman God found more faith than in all the bishops, princes, priests, and all the people of the Jews. . . . [W]ith great eloquence, the Samaritan woman spoke well on her own behalf when she went to the well to draw water and met Jesus Christ. . . . You did not in the least disdain the pious sex of women. God, how often would our contemporary pontiffs deign to discuss anything with some simple little woman, let alone her own salvation?[8]

Christine is also instructed about the noble, virtuous, intelligent, learned, and inventive women in history. Woven in among many women from classical antiquity and medieval European history are a few women from the Hebrew scriptures: Judith, Esther, Susanna, Sarah, Rebecca, Ruth. Among the Christian saints and martyrs are only a few women from the New Testament: Mary Magdalene and, of course, the Virgin Mary, Queen of Heaven, and her sisters. All these virtuous women will come to live in the City of Ladies.[9]

Christine used very sophisticated literary devices to reveal a self-consciousness remarkable for that period about the oppression of women, their life under "Pharaoh," the "lies and ignorance" of the philosophers and theologians about women, and the damage these burdens inflict on women's dignity and self-confidence. A Renaissance influence is clear from the numerous allusions to and appropriations of Greek and Roman history/mythology and philosophy and from the critical use of reason to test and shape tradition. Her carefully studied portrait of Jesus as respectful of women is significant for the tradition of women's advocacy. She intentionally selected the scriptural texts she used to show the dignity and worthiness of women. In this book and others by Christine, however, the social roles of women remain quite traditional.

Marguerite, Queen of Navarre

Marguerite ruled over her own lands as Queen of Navarre, but she also played an important role at the court in Paris as the influential sister of King Francis I of France. She was a serious writer, especially of poetry and drama. In all of these roles she was caught up in the religious controversies of the early sixteenth century. Though she remained Catholic all her life, she was significantly involved with the Catholic humanist reforming movements in France, and she was interested in Protestantism. She invited Protestant pastors to preach at court, protected Protestants in danger of the inquisition, and translated one of Luther's writings into French. She also played a role in the debate about women, defending women.

After her death in 1549, *The Heptameron*[10] was published, a work that is attributed to Marguerite. The format is a collection of short stories, supposedly true, told by a party of noblemen and women to while away their time while trapped by floodwaters at a monastery. Probably the tales were collected, not written, by Marguerite and shaped by her into a framework of interpretation. The theme is the relation of women and men, sometimes amorous, sometimes murderous. Many stories tell in excruciating detail of the mistreatment of women by men, often Franciscans. Still, men and women are both portrayed sometimes as good, sometimes as sinful. Women are commended in some stories for being strong and clever in out-witting lecherous men, and they are criticized in other stories for being ex-ploited on account of their timidity or too-trusting nature.[11]

A revealing part of the format is the discussion among the men and women after each of the stories, revealing their attitudes toward the sto-ries. The dialogue following story 67 takes up a theme familiar in writings of the reforming women—the importance of looking broadly at scripture, and especially at Paul's writings, not just repeating commands for women to be silent. Here a man begins the dialogue:

> "Now ladies, will you not admit that I have fairly praised the virtues that the Lord has endowed you with—virtues which are all the worthier to be praised as their recipients are the weaker?"
>
> "Far be it from us," replied Oisille, "to be sorry that you praise the graces of Our Lord in us, for in truth all goodness flows from Him; but it must be avowed that neither man nor woman is favoured in the work of God, for in their endeavours, both do but plant, and God alone gives the increase."
>
> "If you've read Scripture properly," said Saffredent, "you will know that Saint Paul wrote that Apollos planted and that he watered, but he says nothing about *women* lending a hand in God's labour!"
>
> "You're as bad as all the other men who take a passage from Scrip-ture which serves their purposes, and leave out anything that contradicts it. If you had read everything Saint Paul says, you would find that he commends himself to those women who have laboured with him in the Gospel."[12]

The last speaker may well be referring to the last chapter of Romans with its long list of women as well as men co-workers, headed by Phoebe the deacon.

Though the group of noble travelers is sheltered in a monastery, and they attend mass and vespers with the monks, the monks are portrayed as corrupt and lacking in spirituality. The travelers prevail on Oisille to allow them to share her daily Bible study. Thus a devout older woman, inspired by the Holy Spirit, accustomed to reading the Bible and singing the psalms, becomes their teacher. She teaches them from Romans and the Epistle of John as well as the Pentecost story, and the other not no-ticeably devout travelers speak with increasing enthusiasm as the days go by about how interesting and spiritual the lessons are and how quickly the hour passes.[13] The group's respect for the ability of Oisille, the pious laywoman, to communicate the power of the Word of God stands in stark contrast to the disrespect for the impious monks who should have been their spiritual guides.

I think there was a connection in Marguerite's mind between the debate quoted above about the role of women in the early church and the way she wove a woman's teaching ministry into the life of this ephemeral community.

Marie Dentière

In 1536, Marie Dentière published the first history of the Genevan reformation.[14] Her book is really more a theology of history than a detailed narrative, focusing on the power of the preaching of the Word of God to liberate the city oppressed by its ruthless and brutal neighbor, the Duke of Savoy, and to transform it into a just and peaceful city. God's free mercy has delivered the city by grace alone, without any human merit. It is noteworthy for our purposes that in this book Marie seems sensitive to the women in scripture, pairing Abraham and Sarah, Zechariah and Elizabeth.[15]

It is in Marie's second book, however, that we find self-conscious discussion of the reading of scripture from a woman's perspective. In 1539, Marie published an open letter to Marguerite, Queen of Navarre, ostensibly replying to her inquiry about the situation in Geneva. This book was officially confiscated. In it, Marie is sharply critical of the new pastors appointed in Geneva after the exile of Calvin and his colleagues. She complains that they are too weak and compliant to the city authorities. But she also complains that those to whom God has given grace to write, speak, preach, and announce what Jesus and the apostles did and preached are often rejected and reproved, especially by the learned sages. Those rejected seem to be women.[16] She tells the Queen, "That which God has given you, and revealed to us women, we should not hide and bury in the earth any more than men should. And although it is not permitted to us to preach in public assemblies and churches, it is nonetheless not forbidden to write and admonish one another, in all charity."[17]

Marie's frustration reflects the change in the situation of the church in Geneva. In the years just before Geneva adopted the Protestant Reform in 1536, Marie had been active in missionary work in Geneva. According to a nun in Geneva, Jeanne de Jussie, Marie had come to the convent to preach in an effort to convert the nuns to Protestantism. At least one other woman, Claudine Levet, was also preaching in Geneva.[18] But after the Reformation was organized in 1536, women disappear from the public service of the church. Marie, however, read the parable of the talents as evidence that she and others should not cease to use their gifts in the church's service.

Marie's understanding of the gospel is very inclusive, and she writes:

I ask, did not Jesus die as much for the poor ignorant people and idiots as for my lords who are shaven, tonsured, and mitred? Did he only say: Go, preach my gospel to my lords the wise and great doctors? Did he not say: to all? Do we have two gospels, one for men and the other for women? One for the wise and the other for the foolish? Are we not one in our Lord? In whose name are we baptized, that of Paul or Apollos, of the Pope or of Luther? Is it not in the name of Christ? Certainly he is not at all divided.[19]

This open letter to Queen Marguerite of Navarre gives evidence of some acquaintance with the tradition of the debate about women that we have discussed. The most striking evidence is the section titled "Defense for Women" inserted between the preface and the letter proper. Women had been accused of being too bold in writing one another about scripture. Marie argues here, however, that the women who have written and been named in scripture are not considered too bold, for they are praised for their faith and doctrine as well as their way of life. Sarah and Rebecca are good examples, but the best of all in the Old Testament is the mother of Moses, who dared to keep her son from death, defying the king's edict. Deborah [Delbora], who judged the people of Israel in the time of the Judges, is not to be despised. Marie does not think Ruth should be condemned for having her story in scripture, for she is in Christ's genealogy. And what wisdom the Queen of Sheba must have had to be named both in the Old Testament and by Jesus among the other wise persons.[20]

She writes that the greatest grace given to creatures was given to the Virgin Mary, mother of Jesus, and much grace also was given to Elizabeth. And, she asks, "What preacher [prescheresse] has been made greater than the Samaritan woman, who had no shame at all to preach Jesus and his word, confessing him openly before everyone, as soon as she had heard from Jesus that it is necessary to worship God in spirit and truth (John 4)." Then, she continues, there is the appearance of the resurrected Lord to Mary Magdalene, and the command to the other women by the angel to go preach and declare the resurrection.[21]

Marie admits that women have their faults, but, she notes, it was not a woman who betrayed Jesus or who invented ceremonies and heresies, but men!

> If then God has given graces to some good women, revealing to them by the Holy Scriptures something holy and good, will they not dare to write, speak, or declare it one to the other for fear of despisers of truth? Ah! This would be too boldly done to wish to stop them, and for us, it would be too foolishly done to hide the talent which God has given us. May God give us grace to persevere to the end. Amen![22]

Once again Marie evokes the parable of the talents to explain why women should not cease to use the gifts of grace God gives. She also uses the story of the Samaritan woman at the well and the resurrection story to claim Jesus' authority for women to "preach."

These were not the messages received from scripture by the male leaders of Geneva. The pastors who had replaced Calvin and his colleagues expressed great frustration at the women who were daring to discuss the French Bible and accuse the pastors.[23] Calvin himself was careful to explain that the Samaritan woman did well in sharing her new faith with others, but she did not assume for herself the role of teacher.[24] Certainly she was not a "preacher"! Calvin at times seems to acknowledge a brief mandate to the women at the tomb to teach, as a punishment to the fearful disciples, but that mandate had long ceased.[25]

Argula von Grumbach

Argula seems to have come into contact with Lutheranism quite early, and she became well acquainted with Martin Luther and other reformers. Her sons and a daughter studied in various Lutheran centers. She was concerned about rising persecution in the Netherlands and in Hungary when in 1522 the court in Munich banned Lutheranism. At the University of Ingolstadt, serious efforts were made to seek out any evidence of Lutheran "heresy." Among the students was Arsacius Seehofer, a young man from a respected local family who had visited Wittenberg, attended lectures on the Bible, and returned with Lutheran sympathies and with writings of Luther and Melanchthon. He was arrested and his errors were laid out by a theological commission. Despite some protests within the university community, Seehofer was pressured into recanting publicly before the university in order to limit his punishment to confinement in a monastery.[26]

About two weeks later, on September 20, 1523, Argula von Grumbach wrote the University of Ingolstadt to protest, creating an angry uproar. She wanted to debate the university, to hear them defend their condemnation of Luther. She announced that though she did not know Latin, they could use German. As a result of her challenge, her husband was dismissed from his position, creating major family problems, and Argula was vilified. She continued to write and publish until the autumn of 1524. By the time her publishing career began, she had become a serious student of the Bible, and her writings are filled with a wide range of biblical citations.[27]

Her letter to the university is bold and confident. Why did she presume to write such a letter? What message did she find in scripture? First, she believed that this crisis was a time for confession. She believed that Luther's theology was biblical theology. Thus, to deny Luther's teaching was to deny God's word. There had been no refutation of his position, and she did not find in the Bible that Christ imprisoned, burned, murdered, or exiled people.[28]

I find there is a text in Matthew 10 which runs: "Whoever confesses me before another I too will confess before my heavenly Father." And Luke 9: "Whoever is ashamed of me and of my words, I too will be ashamed of when I come in my majesty," etc. Words like these, coming from the very mouth of God, are always before my eyes. For they exclude neither woman nor man.

And this is why I am compelled as a Christian to write to you. For Ezekiel 33 says: "If you see your brother sin, reprove him, or I will require his blood at your hands."[29]

Argula felt a corporate responsibility toward the people of God for the Word of God. She reported the prophets' judgments on those who would not listen.

She had already made clear that women are as responsible for confession as are men. Yet she was still aware of the problem of a woman speaking:

However I suppressed my inclinations; heavy of heart, I did nothing. Because Paul says in 1 Timothy 2: "The women should keep silence, and should not speak in church." But now that I cannot see any man who is up to it, who is either willing or able to speak, I am constrained by the saying: "Whoever confesses me," as I said above. And I claim for myself Isaiah 3: "I will send children to be their princes; and women, or those who are womanish, shall rule over them."[30]

Once again, the obligation to confess the faith overrode the considerations of Paul's command for women's silence. And Isaiah 3 is a classic text justifying extraordinary action when men are not available or are found wanting.

As with Marie Dentière, the parable of the talents also spoke to Argula, and she wrote, "I don't intend to bury my talent, if the Lord gives me grace."[31] She believed God had given her insights of faith that required activity in behalf of truth.

Beseeching the university for a reply, she cited the example of the great fourth-century biblical scholar, Jerome: "I beseech and request a reply from you if you consider that I am in error, though I am not aware of it. For Jerome was not ashamed of writing a great deal to women, to Blesilla, for example, to Paula, Eustochium and so on."[32] Then she added the example of Christ, as had Christine de Pisan: "Yes, and Christ himself, he who is the only teacher of us all, was not ashamed to preach to Mary Magdalene, and to the young woman at the well."[33]

In her closing argument Argula wrote, "What I have written to you is no woman's chit-chat, but the word of God; and (I write) as a member of the Christian Church, against which the gates of Hell cannot prevail."[34] Once more, her membership in the church and her obligation to confess took precedence.

Argula sent a copy of her letter explaining her actions both to the university and to the Council of Ingolstadt. She appealed in that cover letter to her baptism and invoked Joel 2:28, so familiar in writings supporting women:

> Therefore call to mind the vow which you made to God at baptism, which states: "I believe, and renounce all the pomp and illusions of the Devil. . . ." [T]o be a Christian means to resist as best we can those who would condemn the word of God; not with weapons, though, but rather with the word of God. . . . What doctor [of theology] could be so learned that his vow is worth more than mine? The Spirit of God is promised to me as much as to him. As God says in Joel 2: "I will pour out my Spirit upon all flesh, and your sons and daughters will prophesy."[35]

Conclusion

From this brief survey of writings of reforming women, we see two major polemical themes, two different messages, arising from their reading of scripture—the dignity of women and responsibility. In the earliest examples, the focus is on the dignity of women, made in the image of God, and on their demonstrated accomplishments. Though this theme continues to be stressed, in the Protestant writers the theme of responsibility emerges clearly. Marie Dentière and Argula von Grumbach were convinced that God calls on women and men alike to confess their faith publicly, even at great risk, and to use the gifts and graces entrusted to them in God's service. They internalized the Protestant teaching of the priesthood of all believers more radically than did their male pastors.

Notes

1. For further discussion of this group of writers from another perspective, see Jane D. Douglass, "Anticlericalism in Three French Women Writers, 1404–1539," in *Anticlericalism in Late Medieval and Early Modern Europe,* ed. Peter A. Dykema and Heiko A. Oberman (Leiden: E. J. Brill, 1993), 243–56.
2. For the nature of this debate about women, see Joan Kelly, *Women, History, and Theory* (Chicago: University of Chicago Press, 1984), chap. 4.
3. For Christine's biography, see Charity Cannon Willard, *Christine de Pizan: Her Life and Works* (New York: Persea Books, 1984).
4. Christine de Pizan, *The Book of the City of Ladies,* trans. Earl Jeffrey Richards (New York: Persea Books, 1982), 4.
5. Ibid., 4–5.
6. Ibid., 10; see 6–10.
7. Ibid., 23; see 16–24.
8. Ibid., 26–30.

9. Ibid., 142–45, 155–57, 217–19.
10. Marguerite de Navarre, *The Heptameron,* trans. P. A. Chilton (New York: Penguin Books, 1984).
11. Ibid., Stories 5 and 46 (pp. 98–101, 406–9); stories 46 and 72 (pp. 406–9, 540–43).
12. Ibid., 505.
13. See, for example, ibid., 66–67, 69, 155, 235, 324, 376, 428.
14. For further information on Marie, see Jane Dempsey Douglass, "Marie Dentière's Use of Scripture in Her Theology of History," in *Biblical Hermeneutics in Historical Perspective,* ed. Mark S. Burrows and Paul Rorem (Grand Rapids: Wm. B. Eerdmans, 1991), 227–44.
15. Text in Albert Rilliet, ed., "Restitution de l'écrit intitulé: La guerre et deslivrance de la ville de Genesve (1536),"*Mémoires et documents publiés par la Société d'histoire et d'archéologie de Genève* 20 (1881), 340–41. Brief excerpts of both of Marie Dentière's writings can be found in Thomas Head, "Marie Dentière: A Propagandist for the Reform," in *Women Writers of the Renaissance and Reformation,* ed. Katharina M. Wilson (Athens: University of Georgia Press, 1987), 260–83.
16. *Epistre très utile faicte et composée par une femme Chrestienne de Tornay, Enuoyée à la Royne de Nauarre seur du Roy de France. Contre Lés Turcz, Iuifz, Infideles, Faulx chrestiens, Anabaptistes, & Lutheriens* (Anuers [actually Geneva], 1539), in A.-L. Herminjard, *Correspondance des réformateurs dans les pays de langue française* (Geneva, 1878), 5:296–97.
17. *Epistre,* in Herminjard, 5:297–98.
18. Jane Dempsey Douglass, *Women, Freedom, and Calvin* (Philadelphia: Westminster Press, 1985), 100–102.
19. *Epistre,* in Herminjard, 383.
20. Ibid., 378–79.
21. Ibid., 379.
22. Ibid., 379–80.
23. Herminjard, 5:217.
24. Calvin, *Commentary on John, CO,* 47, 92.
25. See the discussion in Douglass, *Women, Freedom, and Calvin,* 58–59.
26. Peter Matheson, ed., *Argula von Grumbach: A Woman's Voice in the Reformation* (Edinburgh: T. & T. Clark, 1995), 7–16. This volume has substantial introductions and translations of the texts of all the surviving writings of Argula.
27. Ibid., 17–23.
28. Ibid., 75–77.
29. Ibid., 75.
30. Ibid., 79.
31. Ibid., 87.
32. Ibid., 88.
33. Ibid.
34. Ibid., 90.
35. Ibid., 118–19.

Part II

Gender Issues in the
Life of the Christian Community

7

Vocation, Motherhood, and Marriage

Rich man, poor man, beggar man, thief.
Doctor, lawyer, merchant, chief.
A tinker, a tailor, a cowboy, a sailor.
A butcher, a baker, a candlestick maker.
—Nursery rhyme

When I was in elementary school, my girl friends and I recited this rhyme to correspond with each button we were wearing that day. When we came to our last button, the rhyme indicated what occupation our future husband would have. Although we didn't really believe that our fate was set for life by the number of buttons we wore, it was upsetting when the rhyme ended on "thief" (a husband we would rather avoid) and confusing when it stopped at "tinker" (an occupation we didn't really understand). What is curious to me now, of course, is that we never used the rhyme or counted buttons to determine our *own* vocations. We were more concerned about whom we would marry than who we would be.

By the time I went to college in the early 1970s, that had changed. By then, becoming a doctor or a lawyer was more important for many women than marrying one. Traditional vocations for women like teacher and nurse were initially avoided, because for so many years those were the only careers open to us. Eventually we came to believe that the real issue was choice, and now that women had a variety of options, traditional vocations could be freely chosen as well—every traditional vocation, that is, except full-time homemaker, for not only had our ideas about careers changed, so had our thoughts about marriage and motherhood.

Even though a popular saying at the time ("A woman without a man is like a fish without a bicycle") conveyed an exhilarating sense of independence, most of the women I knew still thought (a lot) about dating and marriage. Our visions of marriage and motherhood, however, challenged the hierarchically structured family in which husbands were the heads of households and women were dutiful "housewives." We developed instead an egalitarian view of marriage where husbands and wives divided household chores between them, honored each other's vocational commitments, and shared the duties of parenthood equally.

Although many of our ideas were naive (most of us knew little about marriage or motherhood), we were, nevertheless, part of a widespread cultural movement in this country that challenged rigid distinctions in vocation between men and women as well as any ranked order between them. As a result of that movement, women have made significant inroads into what once were entirely male professions, more families have seen fathers taking greater responsibility for fundamental elements of child care and domestic chores, and more women have had the freedom to pursue vocations in addition to (or other than) motherhood.

Some people today, however, believe that this same cultural movement, which freed women to cultivate their gifts and interests, has contributed to the rise in the divorce rate, the unhealthy leveling of distinctions between males and females, and the devaluation of motherhood. For them, rebuilding the two-parent nuclear family provides the only way to address the pressing problems of our society. Accordingly, men should again be given primary authority in the family, and women should be recognized as the most significant caregivers for the child. Although the conservative evangelicals who lead this movement challenge fathers to be more involved in the lives of their children than they were traditionally, they, nevertheless, support a return to the traditional hierarchical relationship between husbands and wives and renewed respect for the traditional role of motherhood.

This chapter explores how the doctrine of vocation addresses issues of gender as they relate to motherhood and to the appropriate relational structure between men and women in marriage. First I explore the significance of the doctrine of vocation for addressing the tension that has arisen between mothers who are full-time homemakers and mothers with careers. Then I challenge both the hierarchical structure of relationship between men and women (promoted by such evangelical leaders as James Dobson) and the egalitarian one (which once seemed so promising to many of us), before proposing an alternative structure of belonging based on the concept of reciprocal responsibility. Finally, I describe four elements of a Christian sexual ethic regarding gender relations and motherhood.[1]

Motherhood

Full-Time Homemakers

Critics of the women's movement rightly claim that in its early stages it devalued motherhood by urging women to forsake family for careers.[2] Although Betty Friedan, in her 1963 book *The Feminist Critique,* for instance, rightly uncovered the unhappiness of many women who were asked to forsake everything for their families, she left the impression that being a full-time homemaker is never a viable alternative for any self-respecting woman.[3] Over thirty years after the publication of Friedan's book, full-time homemakers feel that few people value the effort they put into building an environment where their children can thrive. They are instead accused of wasting their time and talents by not pursuing a career.

Even the language used to describe women who have chosen mother-hood over employment tends at best to be inaccurate. The older term *housewife* and the contemporary term *stay-at-home mom* suggest that full-time homemakers rarely venture beyond the house. Even the phrase *full-time homemaker* suggests that these mothers spend most of their time at home. In reality, not only does motherhood require one to leave the con-fines of home, full-time homemakers are often more active in their local communities than mothers with careers. In addition to the inaccurate na-ture of the terms *housewife* and *stay-at-home mom,* the designation of *working mother* to describe mothers with careers is also insulting to full-time homemakers, for it implies that they do not work. Anyone who takes care of small children or tends to the needs of teenagers knows, as pop-ular artist and poet Mary Englebreit does, that "all mothers are working women."

Mothers with Careers

Ironically, mothers with careers discover that their choice is also dis-paraged. They find themselves accused of "wanting it all" (an accusation never leveled against men who have vocations alongside fatherhood) and, worse, of neglecting their children for the sake of career. Furthermore, the workplace is structured for workers without children or for men whose wives are full-time homemakers. The forty-hour-per-week, fifty-week-per-year work schedule fails to address the needs of most families. Benefits such as maternity leave, paternity leave, on-site day care, job sharing, and flexible hours that support mothers (and fathers) in the workplace are rarely readily available. Home life, on the other hand, is so highly privat-ized that domestic responsibilities, including child care, remain the sole responsibility of parents, especially mothers. In fact, mothers often labor under a "double work day," managing one day's labor at work and an-other at home.

The Doctrine of Vocation

The lack of support experienced by both full-time homemakers and mothers with careers reveals a fundamental disrespect for all mothers and for the task of taking care of children. We need to stop dictating how the

Nancy J. Duff

vocation of motherhood must be fulfilled always in the same way and instead discover the means for supporting mothers whose situations vary. The doctrine of vocation redirects our energies in such a manner. Four fundamental aspects of the doctrine of vocation important for our purposes are these: (1) each individual has divinely appointed purpose; (2) we are called to glorify God in all that we do; (3) we are to help provide others with an environment suitable for glorifying God; and (4) the freedom of God preserves the integrity of vocational differences.[4]

1. *Each individual life has divinely appointed purpose.* John Calvin makes this affirmation as he reflects on the wonder of childbirth:

> Although it is by the operation of natural causes that infants come into the world . . . yet therein the wonderful providence of God brightly shines forth. This miracle, it is true, because of its ordinary occurrence, is made less account of by us. But if ingratitude did not put upon our eyes the veil of stupidity, we would be ravished with admiration at every childbirth in the world.[5]

The doctrine of vocation claims that each human life matters. Like Mordecai addressing Esther, we can say to each other, "And who knows whether you have not come to the kingdom for such a time as this?" (Esth. 4:14; RSV). Although human sin often thwarts our divinely appointed purpose, it does not destroy the value God bestows on each individual.

2. *We are called to glorify God in all that we do.* Although the doctrine of vocation is often limited to the workplace, it actually encompasses every area of our lives. Our most fundamental vocation, as the catechism teaches, is to "glorify God and enjoy [God] forever." If we relegate vocation solely to the workplace, then people who are too old or too young to work, or who work at something other than paid employment, would be told they have no divinely appointed vocation. By contrast, Luther believed that all tasks can be done to the glory of God.

> Now you tell me, when a father goes ahead and washes diapers or performs some other mean task for his child, and someone ridicules him as an effeminate fool—though that father is acting . . . in Christian faith—my dear fellow you tell me, which of the two is most keenly ridiculing the other. God, with all his angels and creatures, is smiling—not because that father is washing diapers, but because he is doing so in Christian faith.[6]

Of course, this affirmation of our freedom to glorify God in every task we perform would be distorted if turned into law. If we were compelled to glorify God no matter how dreary or demeaning our task, our vocation would become an unbearable burden rather than an expression of Christian freedom.

3. *We are called to provide an arena in which others can express their divinely appointed purpose.* Although the doctrine of vocation has been

misused to counsel tolerance for oppressive situations, if rightly interpreted it challenges oppressive conditions. The church is commissioned to change those structures that prevent people from fulfilling their divine vocation. Hence, we need to ensure in both the workplace and the home that women, men, and children have an arena in which it is possible to glorify God and to fulfill their divinely appointed purpose in life.

4. *The doctrine of vocation challenges arguments that deny the freedom of God to call people to different identities and tasks.* Identical roles cannot be assigned to all members of any one race, class, culture, or gender. Not all women are called to be mothers, nor all men to be fathers; some women are called to the ordained ministry, and some men into full-time child care. God calls each individual into a vocation which matches that person's gifts and graces.

Vocation and Motherhood

These four aspects of the doctrine of vocation significantly influence our understanding of motherhood.[7] First, the doctrine of vocation celebrates women's ability to conceive, bear, and nurture children without making it a requirement for achieving "true womanhood." Women are not required to choose motherhood to fulfill their vocation as women. Women's vocation is not defined biologically; that is, because we *can* conceive, bear, and nurture children, therefore we *must*. Furthermore, because God calls each woman to tasks that fit her gifts, there are many ways to fulfill one's vocation as mother.

Instead of defining a set pattern that all mothers must take, the doctrine of vocation recognizes the need to match the gifts and abilities of mothers with the individual needs of their children in the specific situation in which they live. Hence, both the expectation that mothers *must abandon careers* and the expectation that mothers *must have careers* are equally unfair. Some women best fulfill their vocation as mothers by spending the major portion of every day focused on their children. Other women find that both they and their children do better when they can direct some of their attention toward a vocation in addition to motherhood.

Furthermore, some mothers have the economic privilege of leaving aside employment to tend to their children, whereas others must work to survive financially. Ironically, some upper-middle-class mothers are criticized for pursuing careers, while "welfare mothers" are criticized for not seeking employment.[8] Arguing against any single ideal imposed on motherhood, the doctrine of vocation calls us to support mothers from all economic, cultural, and social settings, addressing the needs of single and married mothers, of poor and economically privileged mothers, of full-time homemakers and mothers with careers. Rather than dictating which route mothers should choose (careers or full-time homemaking), our attention should be focused on the well-being of all mothers and children by advocating peaceful means of childrearing, curtailing domestic violence, addressing the effects of poverty on families, and restructuring the workplace to serve the needs of employees and their families.

For all the political bantering about "family values," we live in a society that does not value children. We are caught between romanticizing motherhood and the family and holding the institutions of motherhood and family in contempt. At one time, the romanticization of motherhood was reflected in popular television shows such as *Father Knows Best,* where in the "ideal" family fathers had careers while mothers were full-time homemakers—an ideal that sharply divides the poor from the privileged, and private home life from public work life. Today the offensive, but popular, *Married with Children* portrays parents and children holding each other in mutual contempt and reduces values to individual choice and self-gratification. Neither image provides what families need to sustain a humanizing ethos. The doctrine of vocation and the freedom of God to call individuals into identities, tasks, and patterns of relationship that fit their particular contexts tolerate neither a rigid structure whereby all families must be configured in the same way nor a chaotic focus on fulfilling individual needs.

The Structure of Male-Female Relationships

> Man for the field and woman for the hearth;
> Man for the sword and for the needle she;
> Man with the head and woman with the heart;
> Man to command and woman to obey;
> All else confusion.[9]

A number of Christians in the latter part of the twentieth century can be just as certain as Alfred, Lord Tennyson was in the nineteenth that men and women were created with such different physical, spiritual, and emotional dispositions that different vocational arenas are appropriately assigned to each. Taking their cue from biological differences and from biblical texts, they also promote a ranked order between the sexes that results in a complementary but hierarchical structure of relationship where men have an authority women cannot claim. Over the past thirty years, however, other Christians have challenged these distinctions in vocation between women and men as well as the rank ordering of authority between them. Taking their cue from the similarities between women and men and from alternative biblical texts, they promote a more egalitarian structure of relationship between men and women. In this section I challenge the "complementary but hierarchical" relationship between men and women that is promoted by conservative evangelicals such as James Dobson.[10] I also challenge the egalitarian perspective and promote instead an understanding of reciprocal responsibility.

Hierarchical Structure

Conservative evangelical Christians in America today advocate distinctions between the vocations of men and women that they believe are borne out by the biological differences. They promote the restoration and protection of the two-parent, nuclear family where the husband exercises leadership and the wife feels supported and loved. This return to the "traditional" structure of the family is for them critical to the stability of America. These evangelical Christians are represented in all major denominations, are predominantly Republican, and through carefully organized groups seek through the political process to put their agenda before the rest of America. These groups include the Christian Coalition led by Ralph Reed, Phyllis Schlafly's Eagle Forum, and James Dobson's "Focus on the Family" with its nationally syndicated radio program.[11]

These evangelical conservatives address problems that also concern feminists, such as the abandonment of women and children by their husbands and fathers, the rise in domestic abuse, and the mistreatment of victims of violent crime. An enormous gulf exists, however, between the way feminists and conservative evangelicals view the causes of these problems. Conservative evangelicals blame the rise in child abuse in large part on the children's rights movement, while laying poverty and crime at the door of single-parent families. The present instability of the American family and the resulting confusion regarding men's and women's roles are largely blamed on the women's movement of the 1960s.

James Dobson provides one of the leading voices for this "pro-family" movement. With a background as a professor of clinical pediatrics, his numerous books seek to help families strengthen marriages, discipline children, resolve conflict, and gain spiritual health. Founder and president of "Focus on the Family," his nationally syndicated radio program is broadcast on more than fifteen hundred radio stations. Like other conservative evangelical Christians, Dobson believes that the nuclear family is critical to the well-being of America. He also claims that the only relationship between husband and wife that adequately sustains the nuclear family is one that is complementary but hierarchical.

According to Dobson, women's natural ability to nurture coupled with men's ability to protect, together with women's need for stability and the male ego's need to be in charge, create a complementary relationship where women and men each provide what the other needs.[12] Dobson argues that the natural predispositions of men and women are corrected and enhanced through the appropriate relationship between them. For instance, he claims that as a group, single men pose a threat to society. They are responsible for the majority of violent crimes, burglaries, drunken-driving incidences, and violent offenses against children.[13] Because of women's commitment to children, they, in contrast, are more inclined toward the stability necessary for building a home. When the destructive tendencies of single men are coupled with the desire for stability exhibited by women, a marriage made in heaven results. According to Dobson, men were created, physically and emotionally, to be protector and provider to their wives and children. Undermining the husband's role as head of the family poses a serious threat to the family, for if this role is destroyed, a man's commitment to his wife and children is jeopardized.[14] Hence, Dobson aims strong criticism against men who have deserted their families through divorce or by pouring all of their time into work; nevertheless, when he encourages men to return to their responsibilities, he intends them to assume their proper role as leaders.

Dobson believes that God holds men responsible for every aspect of family life:

> God expects a man to be the ultimate decision maker in his family. Likewise, he bears heavier responsibility for the outcome of those decisions. If his family has purchased too many items on credit, then the financial crunch is ultimately his fault. If the family never reads the Bible or seldom goes to church, God holds the man to blame. If the children are disrespectful and disobedient, the primary responsibility lies with the father . . . not his wife.[15]

Although Dobson admits that some couples have successfully followed a different structure of cooperation, he believes that marriages falter when the man lacks qualities of leadership. According to him, "none of the modern alternatives have improved on the traditional, masculine role" that he believes is prescribed in the Bible.[16] If men abdicate their leadership role, the family will subsequently disintegrate, just as the corporation will collapse if its president ceases to exercise authority.

Dobson does not intend to claim that women are of less value than men. He insists that being different from men does not make women inferior.[17] Furthermore, he recognizes that "submission to masculine leadership does not extend . . . to behaviors that will be unhealthy for the husband, the wife, and the marriage. Nor should a woman tolerate child abuse, child molestation, or wife-beating."[18] In fact, Dobson's work often exhibits great compassion for the plight of women trapped in unhappy marriages. Unfortunately, however, he offers them little relief by failing to recognize that his position gives men all the advantages. While men are called upon to take a lion's share of the responsibility, they have the authority for making all major decisions and for doing things *their* way. Dobson suggests that only two choices face the American family: allowing men to neglect their families or allowing them to control them. He readily admits that the latter position feeds the "fragile male ego" and "man's enormous need to be respected."[19] He also admits that this is simply the way he—and presumably other men—like things to be.

In Dobson's position, hierarchy outweighs complementarity. He has forged a bond between privilege and power, assigning both to men. Dobson fails to recognize that in every relationship between a man and a woman, there needs to be give-and-take regarding authority and power. The circumstances, dispositions, and needs of both a man and a woman may indeed require the man to take the lead. But in other circumstances, the woman may need to exercise more power. In marriage, for instance, there may be times when the wife needs the husband to take over, make decisions, and carry a greater burden. At other times, however, the husband may feel his energies spent, his burden overwhelming, and the wife takes the lead. At still other times, there may be an equal reserve of energy and hopefulness, and they proceed with no need to distinguish sequence or authority. Dobson's position denies the need for this give-and-take within marriage.

Furthermore, although Dobson rightly affords genuine dignity to mothers and homemakers, the respect women are given is patronizing and finally debilitating. (In one case he advises women whose husbands neglect them to find solace in one another, for they cannot change their husbands.)[20] Dobson also puts more weight on the individual nuclear family than it can possibly bear. Poverty and racism, for instance, are ignored as factors contributing to the instability of America. Rebuilding the two-parent nuclear family is viewed as the solution to most societal ills. In reality, individual family units cannot bear the burden of such expectation.

Egalitarianism or Reciprocal Responsibility

Against the views of conservative evangelicals, some Christians propose an egalitarian structure of relationship between men and women. Advocates of this view propose that each person is a human being first. That we are male or female has only secondary significance. Essential differences between men and women are strictly biological; any other differences are strictly socialized. In putting pink clothes on a girl and blue clothes on a boy, giving dolls to girls and trucks to boys, and encouraging different choices in vocation, we teach children and adults what it means to be male or female. We could just as readily teach them to assume different characteristics and roles. In its most extreme form, this position advocates androgyny. In its less radical forms, the terms *masculine* and *feminine* are either identified as distinct traits that, nevertheless, apply to both sexes, or are abolished altogether. This position rightly recognizes that differences exist more distinctly among individuals than between the sexes.

This refusal to acknowledge any distinction between the sexes, however, produces its own set of problems. How can one talk about human beings in general, waiving all distinctions between masculine and feminine, and still refer to anything like "women's experience" or "male attitudes?" Do we further devalue motherhood and sisterhood if we level all distinctions between men and women? Do we risk reinforcing the idea that males set the standard for personhood and women are simply to be like men?

Some women find that the egalitarian ideal has not worked for them. Sylvia Hewlett, for instance, tells a harrowing story of teaching college in the 1960s.[21] When she discovered she was pregnant, the egalitarian ideals of her female colleagues made them insist that she not ask for special privileges as a woman and a mother. (She was finally given a two-week maternity leave.) On the other hand, women she contacted outside the workplace refused to support her when they discovered that she intended to return to work after the birth of her child. Neither the egalitarian vision nor the romanticized vision of motherhood addressed her needs. Hewlett has more recently been deemed an enemy of feminism.[22] Some feminists, however, agree with her assessment of the inadequacy of egalitarianism as a means to promote women's concerns. Women in the workplace sometimes find themselves torn between demanding equality (being treated like men) or insisting on special benefits (recognizing that women's needs are different from men's, but risking the hierarchical structure they seek to avoid).

While both hierarchy and egalitarianism are inadequate structures for addressing the needs of women, each describes an essential aspect of human social interaction.[23] Paul Lehmann, for instance, argues that hierarchy recognizes "differentiation and variation" as a reality in social interaction, whereas egalitarianism recognizes "shared interaction, commonality, and need" as essential to human relatedness. Because each one denies what the other assumes, neither hierarchy nor egalitarianism provides the freedom that being human requires.[24] Furthermore, both hierarchy and egalitarianism bear a fatal flaw. Hierarchy tends to wed privilege with power and therefore too easily results in tyranny and submission. Egalitarianism tends to equate equality with sameness, thereby overlooking essential differences among us. Whereas hierarchy emphasizes the ways we are different, rather than celebrating the ways we are similar, egalitarianism emphasizes the ways we are alike without taking responsibility for the ways we are different.[25]

Seeking a tertium quid between hierarchy and egalitarianism can lead to a structure of relationship between men and women that Paul Lehmann has termed "reciprocal responsibility." Unlike egalitarianism (which insists on reciprocated responsibility), this pattern recognizes the differences in power, needs, gifts, and limitations that exist at various times between a man and a woman. The pattern, however, does not assign power to only one person in the relationship.

Also, a structure of reciprocal responsibility recognizes that in order for a husband and wife to belong to each other in a humanizing context, each individual must have both a centered sense of self as well as the capacity for self-giving. Belonging to another in marriage does not necessitate the notion of two halves becoming one; that is, that men and women are somehow incomplete until finding wholeness in one another. Neither, of course, are they isolated, self-sufficient individuals who simply live side by side. Rather, wives and husbands belong to one another when each whole individual experiences the other whole individual as a gift.

> Belonging is the experience of a relation through which one knows who one is, as and where one is, in what one does. What one does is respond, from a center of unified and stable selfhood, in a free act of self-giving to another self, similarly centered, unified and stable. . . . Belonging is the experience of receiving yourself, as and where you are, as a gift from another who has similarly received you, and finding in everything around you so many different ways of saying "Thank you."[26]

Complementarity between men and women does not require a weaker human being to find completion in the protection of a stronger human being. True complementarity recognizes that a man's and a woman's need for each other is born out of a sense of wholeness, not brokenness.

Concluding Reflections

> Rachel, Rachel, I've been thinking, what a glad world this would be
> If the girls were all transported far beyond the Northern Sea.
> (Nursery rhyme and song)

> Although we adore men individually, we agree that as a group they're rather stupid.
> (Mrs. Banks, in Walt Disney's "Mary Poppins")

Throughout history one finds expressions of deep-seated mistrust and animosity between men and women. If there is not a war between the sexes, there is at least an ongoing skirmish. (Of course, within this conflict men have maintained the greater power to oppress.) I contend that the doctrine of vocation addresses the relationship between men and women in ways that can build mutual trust. The following theses will summarize points already made and seek to lay a foundation for a Christian sexual ethic focused on gender relations and on motherhood.

First, we can use the terms *masculine* and *feminine* and even celebrate the differences between male and female without giving them precise definition. Recognizing certain patterns in men and in women does not necessitate transforming them into rigid expectations. God calls each individual into a particular configuration of gifts, dispositions, and limitations that

79

make each person uniquely who he or she is. We cannot deny someone's divine calling by forcing that person into masculine and feminine roles we have rigidly defined in advance. On the other hand, we affirm that God created humanity male and female—a distinction we celebrate and rightly do not want to negate.

Second, when defining responsible motherhood, we must consider specific situations, individual mothers, and particular children rather than providing one set pattern for all mothers. To claim that all mothers must behave in identical ways denies both the freedom of God and the concrete life situation of mothers, fathers, and their children. If mothers with careers and full-time homemakers could accept the different paths each has been called to take, they could then combine their energies, not only becoming advocates for one another, but for mothers who are overwhelmed by poverty or violence.

Third, neither a hierarchical structure nor an egalitarian one will rightly define our human relatedness as male and female. Just as no single strictly defined pattern exists whereby men and women express their gender, or whereby women are responsible mothers, so no single set pattern defines how men and women should relate to one another. If there is a proper "structure," it must be so fluid that it suits the needs of each individual man and woman and the situation of both together. Belonging and complementarity within marriage do not indicate a superior-subordinate relationship. Men's and women's need for one another should not be borne of desperation or the idea that prior to marriage each is only half a person. Rather, belonging and complementarity occur when a centered self encounters another centered self as gift.

Finally, in every definition of motherhood, fatherhood, and marriage, the best interest of children must be given priority. In our present legal system, the rights of adults often take priority over the best interest of children. Some children are removed from loving foster or adoptive homes and returned to biological parents they have never known or who have previously been abusive. In exploring vocation, motherhood, and marriage, we must challenge the patriarchal idea that children are property and fight against the physical, psychological, and sexual abuse of children worldwide.

Notes

1. I thank Christopher Rogers, a Ph.D. student at Princeton Seminary, for the invaluable assistance he gave in gathering resources for this chapter.
2. Feminist scholars today do address motherhood. See Bonnie F. Miller-McLemore, *Also a Mother: Work and Family as Theological Dilemma* (Nashville: Abingdon Press, 1994).
3. Betty Friedan, *The Feminine Mystique* (New York: W. W. Norton, 1963).
4. Nancy Duff, "Call/Vocation," in *Dictionary of Feminist Theologies,* ed. Letty

M. Russell and J. Shannon Clark (Louisville: Westminster John Knox Press, 1996), 34–35.

5. John Calvin, *Commentary on the Book of Psalms,* trans. James Anderson (Grand Rapids: Baker Book House, 1981 [repro]), I, 369 (on Ps. 22:9).

6. Martin Luther, "The Estate of Marriage" (1522) (German text in *WA* 10 II, 294–96; translated in full in *LW* 45, 17ff.). Cited in *Luther* (New York: Harper & Row, 1972), ed. Ian D. Kingston Siggins, 148–49.

7. See Duff, "Mothers/Motherhood," in *Dictionary of Feminist Theologies,* 186–88.

8. I thank Stephanie Stidham, a Th.M. student at Princeton Seminary, for this observation.

9. Alfred, Lord Tennyson, as cited in Robin Morgan, *Sisterhood Is Powerful: An Anthology of Writings from the Women's Liberation Movement* (New York: Random House, 1970), 33.

10. The designation "complementary but hierarchical" is one of three given by Lisa Cahill in describing the structures of relationship between men and women. The other two are "differentiated but equal" and "equal and interchangeable" (See *Between the Sexes: Foundations for a Christian Ethics of Sexuality* [Philadelphia: Fortress Press, 1985]).

11. These groups were either preceded or established by well-known TV evangelists such as Pat Robertson (founder of the Christian Coalition) and Jerry Falwell (founder of the Moral Majority).

12. James Dobson, *Straight Talk: What Men Need to Know, What Women Should Understand* (Dallas: Word Publishing, 1991), 184.

13. Ibid., 31.

14. Ibid., 26.

15. Ibid., 93.

16. Ibid., 185.

17. Ibid., 179.

18. Ibid., 130.

19. Ibid., 184.

20. Ibid., 135.

21. Sylvia Ann Hewlett, "A Personal View," in *A Lesser Life: The Myth of Women's Liberation in America* (New York: Warner Books, 1987), 18–50.

22. See Susan Faludi, *Backlash: The Undeclared War Against American Women* (New York: Anchor Books, 1992).

23. See Paul Lehmann, *The Decalogue and a Human Future: The Meaning of the Commandments for Making and Keeping Human Life Human* (Grand Rapids: Wm. B. Eerdmans, 1995), esp. chaps. 2 and 3. Lehmann draws on the work of sociologists Peter Blau and Louis Dumont.

24. Ibid., 32.

25. Ibid., 47.

26. Ibid., 218.

8

Women's Ordination:
Can the Church Be Catholic Without It?

A s a deserved right, as a career opportunity, as a statement of civil justice, or as a visibly good work, ordination to the special ministry of Word and sacrament is equally for neither gender. Sin, mere frailty, and creaturely potential are not gender specific. Although that is all true enough, far more true is the fact that grace is not gender specific. As a sacred calling, ordination to the special ministry of Word and sacrament is equally for both genders. Grace is lavishly bestowed on both, including that unmerited favor by which a forgiven female sinner (*simul justa ac peccatrix*) and a forgiven male sinner (*simul justus ac peccator*) are taken up into Christ's own continuing ministry in each of its many forms.

In the following remarks, I want to say more about the implications of this more-than-abundant grace for women and men being equally ordained to the office of pastor and teacher. I will deal, first, with a brief reminder about the context of ordination to the ministry of Word and sacrament; second, with the significance that ordination has in the Reformed tradition; and third, with equal ordination as an effective sign of the new creation in Christ.

The Context of Equal Ordination

The World Council of Churches is "a fellowship of churches which confess the Lord Jesus Christ as God and Saviour according to the scriptures and therefore seek to fulfil together their common calling to the glory of the one God, Father, Son and Holy Spirit."[1]

The context of equal ordination to the ministry of Word and sacrament is the one, holy, catholic, apostolic church.

The document *Baptism, Eucharist and Ministry* was the culmination of years of official dialogues among churches representing widely different traditions. The very first sentence of that document's preface quotes the World Council of Churches' Constitution, which makes it clear that the Council itself is not a church but a fellowship of churches who share a common belief in one God—Father, Son, and Holy Spirit. The presupposition for candid dialogue has always been that shared trinitarian belief; we are able to face serious differences and even to move toward some unexpected agreements because we share a common baptism and a common trinitarian identity.

The World Council of Churches' definition of membership also has the critical significance of identifying what membership is not: It is not membership in a modalistic sect. By this, I refer to the fashionably erroneous expediency of baptizing persons in the name of God the creator, God the redeemer, and God the sanctifier. The Holy Trinity is indeed creator, redeemer, and sanctifier, but those activities do not constitute the threeness of the One who is eternally relational. By equal ordination, women and men are committed to baptize persons in the name of the uniquely Triune—Father, Son, and Holy Spirit. In doing so, men and women commit themselves to transmitting and reinterpreting the apostolic faith and the triune trinitarian structure of the catholic faith.

Reformed Doctrines of Ordination and Consecration

Both *ordination* and *consecration* are terms used in the Reformed tradition, though the various branches may have preferences. *Ordination* tends to emphasize that the act is one of the proper ordering of the gifts of the Spirit for the ministry in which the whole people of God engages. Elevation to a *special ontological status* (whatever that might mean on careful examination) and *hierarchical ordering* are terms frequently used to say what "ordination" does not mean. *Consecration* tends to emphasize that the act is one of setting apart for the exercise of special gifts those who are called to be pastors to Christ's flock. In defining what *consecration* does not mean, supposed "greater holiness" and "sacerdotalism" are the terms frequently used.

Often the Reformed churches have been clearer, and surely more adamant, about what ordination is not than what it is. There is such a historically informed fear of misuses of power and clerical privilege that the positive significance of ordination, or consecration, to the ministry of Word and sacrament seems often lost in a deluge of warnings. It can happen, in some Reformed churches and in some epidemics of polarizing ideologies, that ordination to the special ministry is given so little positive significance that it becomes, in fact, a matter of indifference. Does ordination to the special ministry belong even to the well-being of the church, let alone belonging to the being of the church? If not, then why all the fuss whether anyone be so ordained—men or women or both?

Where there is such a minimal view of ordination to the special ministry (or the functional denial that there is anything at all special about the ministry of Word and sacrament), it is the withholding of ordination that becomes the preoccupation. The focus is not on the doctrine and practice of ordination: The focus is on what is being conveyed to men and women if equality of ordination is not recognized. To use Tillich's language, the dominant symbol becomes not ordination but the withholding of ordination from some. Hence, we have the ironic position of those who, on the one hand, have a minimal view of the special ministry of Word and sacrament, but who, on the other hand, have a maximal view of the injustice perpetuated by opposing equality of women for ordination. If ordination does not mean much (but the refusal of ordination means a great deal), then ordination is already equally unimportant, and time and energy could well be spent debating more lively matters.

On the other hand, such a minimal view of the special ministry of Word and sacrament has not been, nor is it, typical of Reformed churches.[2] If equality of ordination to this office is to be a feature of the future catholicity of the church, then there is an urgent need to recover and further develop the positive meaning of this ordination. Among Reformed church persons there has been a warranted distrust of any doctrine of ordination that would call attention to or "empower" the person himself or herself who is ordained. There has been, however, a far more prominent sense of the high calling, the special gifting, the indispensability and authority of the office of pastor.

That authority is strictly derivative and redefines the nature of authority. The authority of the pastor is not given to a person. The authority of the pastor inheres in the proclamation of the Word to which persons are awesomely called, for which they are marvelously gifted, and for which they are held accountable—to fulfill that particular office in that particular place. Whether in the whole church over the centuries or in one congregation from day to day, the continuity of this special ministry is strictly a matter of the continuity of grace. Certainly, there is structure, polity, discipline to this continuity of grace. Grace matters, and we know this because the Word by whom all was made became flesh. But the reason this continuity is called one of grace is that it is a free gift that we receive moment to moment only because of the continuity of God's steadfast love. Pastoral authority is indeed exercised—but only by those who know the voice of the one pastor, Jesus Christ, and who are thereby continuously freed to be servers, servants, and ministers of that Word.

The foundation of the church's ministry is Christ's own ministry, which is both an accomplished fact and a continuing reality through his Word and Spirit. The order—Christ's ministry and ours—is sharply put in the accounts of Christ's reply to the question of how the disciples will be seated, how they will rank, in the kingdom. It is as they share in Christ's own baptism and drink the cup he drinks; that is, as they share in his own costly servant

Lordship. (See Mark 10:35–45.) The same point is made in the foot washing in John 13:1–19 and then in the threefold question and threefold reply in the risen Christ's dialogue with Peter in John 21:15–19. Christ's ministry is not the cumulative significance of an exceptionally gifted and very, very, very good person who may have been the culmination of the highest of human potential. It is nothing less than the efficacious presence and activity of God manifest in the flesh. Whenever the church suffers amnesia on this point, what it calls its ministry is just the way self-perpetuating religious professionals organize themselves to get done what they think is best for themselves and others. The ministry of Christ is the outworking of the benevolent purposes of the Triune God graciously to be for the world. The mission of Christ is the temporal and spatial going forth of God. The consequent mission of the church is the going forth of those who are joined to Christ and gifted for their life in him by the power of the Holy Spirit.

The call to the ministry is the church's experience of being chosen by God as people who are recipients of the benefits and responsibilities of the new covenant established in Christ. God's presence in Christ creates a reconciled fellowship of those who in turn are ambassadors through whom God extends that reconciliation. (See 2 Cor. 5:11–21.) Even the Gentiles are recipients of the promises made to Abraham, and this is part of the mystery of God's purposes from before the foundation of the world. (See Ephesians 1 and the titles given the people of God in 1 Peter 2:9–10.) The content of the call to ministry is this experience of being chosen and so made a "royal priesthood." In our baptism we accept and covenant to live out that new identity as active participants in Christ's own continual ministry through those joined to him.

The call to a special form of the ministry is the experience of having received particular gifts of the Spirit for the exercise of particular functions within the whole body of Christ. There is indeed an inner call and an outer call to a particular ministry, like the ministry of the Word through preaching and sacrament. The inner call is not open to scrutiny. Vocation to a particular ministry comes, according to the Reformed tradition, as a call from a particular congregation. Exceptions are just that—exceptions.

Ordination or consecration to a particular form of Christ's own ministry is the act by which the community of believers disciplines and orders its life "according to God's Word" by setting apart a person for the exercise of the gifts of the Spirit discerned to be at work in that person. This definition intends to call attention to three components of the significance of ordination.

First, Reformed churches claim to be part of the tradition that uses the phrase "according to the Word of God reformed and always to be reformed Church." That is a somewhat less than fluid translation of *"ecclesia secundum verbum dei reformata et semper reformanda."* The literalness

David Willis

of the translation, however, makes the order of importance clear: Church reform is according to the Word of God. Changes or refusals to change that are not according to the Word of God constitute church deformation. If the phrase "according to the Word of God" is passed over lightly, or if it is complacently assumed, the result is a sect deformed and always to be deformed (*"secta deformata et semper deformanda"*). The "according to the Word" characteristic of reform means that church struggles are not over indifferent matters but over how the church's life and mission are vivified and ordered by the Word, Jesus Christ as witnessed to in the canonical writings of the Old and New Testaments.[3] Hence, we have the weight given in the Reformed heritage to knowledge, fidelity, and congruent skill in the proclamation and teaching that witnesses to Jesus Christ.

Second, as noted above, ordination does not so much convey a power to the person being ordained as it recognizes and validates in public worship the power of the Spirit discernible in that person. Ordination enjoins on the ordinand a particular role within the believing community's discipline. It is a pledge on the person's part and the community's part about how together they are going to seek to attend to the Word. From this societal form of decision, ordination specifies those among the community who are to exercise the public leadership in that central task.

Third, the service of worship in the act of ordination is taken seriously because what renders such a consecration efficacious is the grace of God of which preaching, sacraments, and prayer are ordinary means. That is, worship is comprised of words and actions that are efficacious bearers of God's operative Word.

Calvin's language about the nature and importance of the ministry of the Word is sobering and joyful. It is through persons set apart by Christ to this ministry that the chief governance of the church is exercised, not by any power inherent in them or transferred to them by ordination, but exclusively by virtue of the fact that God chooses them and equips them to teach and preach the doctrine of Christ by which the church lives and by which the church exercises its sole legitimate authority. God through divine "accommodation" makes use of humans as the earthen vessels through whom the Word is spoken again and again. Calvin is speaking of pastors in the *Institutes* 4,3,1, and then goes on, in 4,3,2, to comment about Paul's words in Ephesians 4:8 and 9–10.

> Paul shows by these words that this human ministry which God uses to govern the church is the chief sinew by which believers are held together in one body. He then also shows that the church can be kept intact only if it be upheld by the safeguards in which it pleased the Lord to place its salvation. . . . This is the manner of fulfillment: through the ministers to whom he has entrusted this office and has conferred the grace to carry it out, he dispenses and distributes his gifts to the church; and he shows himself as though present by manifesting the power of his Spirit in this

his institution, that it be not vain or idle. Thus the renewal of the saints is accomplished; thus the body of Christ is built up [Eph. 4:12]; thus "we grow up in every way into him who is the Head" [Eph. 4:15] and grow together among ourselves; thus are we all brought into the unity of Christ, if prophecy flourishes among us, if we receive the apostles, if we do not refuse the doctrine administered to us. Whoever, therefore, either is trying to abolish this order of which we speak and this kind of government, or discounts it as not necessary, is striving for the undoing . . . of the church. For neither the light and heat of the sun, nor food and drink, are so necessary to nourish and sustain the present life as the apostolic and pastoral office is necessary to preserve the church on earth.[4]

This passage describes what Calvin calls the dignity of this form of the ministry. *Dignitas* does not mean the quality of being dignified, but the worth, weight, significance of the office. The worth of the office is simply by grace alone carrying out the task of effectively delivering and retranslating the gospel in subsequent cultures and contexts. There is surely no diminution here of the people of God not ordained to this office. They have their own particular gifts and functions within the body of Christ. Without their exercising their own vocations, the ministry of the whole body of Christ is foreshortened. That they understand their "jobs" as "vocations" of the Living God depends on the presence in their midst of the Word proclaimed through preaching and sacraments.

Rather than being set apart to a status of preferment or position of privilege, pastors who are given this function within the ministry of the whole people of God are set apart to an office of awesome responsibility and accountability. Calvin says there is a "holy, inviolable and perpetual law imposed on" pastors to preach the gospel and to administer the sacraments. He goes on, in the *Institutes* 4,3,6:

But what about the pastors? Paul is speaking not only of himself but of them all when he says, "This is how men should regard us, as ministers of Christ and stewards of the mysteries of God" [1 Cor. 4:1]. Likewise elsewhere: "The bishop must hold to the faithful word, which is, according to the teaching, that he may be able to give instruction in sound doctrine and also to confute those who contradict it" [Titus 1:9]. From these and similar passages which frequently occur, we may infer that in the office of the pastors also there are these two particular functions: to proclaim the gospel and to administer the sacraments. The manner of teaching not only consists in public discourses, but also has to do with private admonitions. . . . [I]t is not my present intention to set forth in detail the gifts of the good pastor, but only to indicate what those who call themselves pastors should profess. That is, they have been set over the church not to have a sinecure but, by the doctrine of Christ to instruct the people to true godliness, to administer the sacred mysteries and to keep and exercise upright discipline. . . . To them all applies what

Paul said of himself: "Woe to me if I do not preach the gospel. . . [since] I am entrusted with a commission" [1 Cor. 9:16–17]. Finally, what the apostles performed for the whole world, each pastor ought to perform for his own flock, to which he is assigned.[5]

This view of the responsibility, the joy in service, of the pastor is reflected in Calvin's treatment not just of the positive aspect of ordination but in his rejection of the misuse and misunderstanding of ordination. His words, in the *Institutes* 4,5,4, are apt for our current practices.

[I]n the Council of Chalcedon . . . it was enacted that there should be no ordinations free of pastoral obligations, that is, that a place be assigned to the person ordained where he is to exercise his office. This decree is very valuable for two reasons. First, that the church may not be burdened with needless expense, and spend upon idle men what ought to be distributed to the poor. Secondly, that those ordained are not to think themselves promoted to an honor but charged with an office which they are with solemn attestation obligated to discharge.[6]

Equality of Ordination as an Effective Sign of the New Creation

Where Christ is present, human barriers are being broken. The Church is called to convey to the world the image of a new humanity. There is in Christ no male or female (Gal. 3:28). Both women and men must discover together their contributions to the service of Christ in the Church. The Church must discover the ministry which can be provided by women as well as that which can be provided by men. A deeper understanding of the comprehensiveness of ministry which reflects the interdependence of men and women needs to be more widely manifested in the life of the Church.

Though they agree on this need, the churches draw different conclusions as to the admission of women to the ordained ministry. An increasing number of churches have decided that there is no biblical or theological reason against ordaining women, and many of them have subsequently proceeded to do so. Yet many churches hold that the tradition of the Church in this regard must not be changed.[7]

This section of *Baptism, Eucharist and Ministry* still concisely summarizes the state of affairs with regard to the ordination of women to the special ministry. That is not good news. It surely is a minimal claim that an increasing number of churches "have decided that there is no biblical or theological reason against ordaining women." There are compelling biblical and theological reasons for ordaining women, and the burden of proof is now on those who refuse to ordain women. Moreover, there is a curiously loose sense of "tradition" in the last sentence of this section: "Yet many churches hold that the tradition of the Church in this regard must not be changed." There is no one "tradition" on this matter. In fact, there are ranges of "the living voice of the Gospel" that demand development for "tradition" to continue to be the faithful transmission of the gospel in successive contexts.

I have mentioned some understandings of ordination that are compelling reasons for ordaining women to the special ministry. Here, I want to lift up one other that has tended to be minimized in much of the discussions leading up to *Baptism, Eucharist and Ministry:* The equal ordination of women and men to the ministry of Word and sacrament is an effective sign of the new creation in Christ. Two other forms of argument have tended to dominate the discussion, the one usually concluding against the ordination of women, and the other usually concluding for it. One argument focuses on the uniqueness of Christ's relation to the Twelve, the other on our common baptism. Both have some validity, but both need the correction that comes with recognizing ordination as an eschatological sign.

The argument from the uniqueness of Christ's relation with the Twelve goes like this. A fundamental power is conveyed in the act of ordination—the power of communicating the grace by which a person is received into the fellowship of the church and restored to it after breaking with that fellowship. To receive this power, a person must be ordained by a person who himself is in the direct and unbroken continuity with the Twelve who themselves received the power of the keys from Christ. A person, man or woman, may surely be an instrument of evangelism, whether ordained or not, and a person may announce the forgiveness of sins and may even say the canon of the mass, whether or not he or she is ordained. But only the ordained priest's words are efficacious in assuring men and women of their forgiveness in the sacrament of reconciliation, and only the ordained priest's words are efficacious in the way the bread and wine become the body and blood of Christ. This power is, of course, not something that either the ordaining agent or the ordained subject control: It is so because Christ himself established the church in this fashion and because Christ is faithful to his promises conveyed to the Twelve. So powerful is this argument from Christ's conveying power to the Twelve for the exercise of this office that it is apparently self-evident to its advocates that only men can be priests because all the apostles were men, and that argument extends to Paul's apostleship.

The argument that focuses on our common baptism goes like this. By baptism all believers are made participants in Christ's own ministry. Women and men by their baptism already share in the only ordination that finally counts—that of the one people of God who commonly constitute the Royal Priesthood. Ordination, consecration, or commissioning is not to a particular office that has continuity in the church; it is an act of practical love by which assignments are made on the basis of verifiable gifts so that the body of Christ may be best organized to carry out its mission. There is nothing finally that is distinctive about the so-called special ministry of Word and sacrament, so why withhold it from women who share, by baptism, the common apostolate?

Focusing on ordination as an effective sign of the new creation in Christ certainly uses material from both arguments, but it is a necessary supplement and corrective to them. Suggestions of it also appear in the above-cited section of the *Baptism, Eucharist and Ministry*. It is familiarly assumed; but, as is the case with many presuppositions, its significance for further development of the doctrine of the ministry is underestimated. It belongs to the future catholicity of the church that the ministry of Word and sacrament (inclusive of the representative priesthood) exhibit, show forth, and be a congruent sign of, the faith we confess: Christ has died, Christ is risen, Christ will come again.

This section refers to the breaking down of barriers, one aspect of the reconciliation Christ has effected between humanity and God, humans and humans, humans and the rest of creation, and a person with herself or himself. Today it is a partial truth, a half-truth, to restrict to males the ordination to the ministry of Word and sacrament, inclusive of the special role of representative intercessor on behalf of all believers who constitute the royal priesthood. The perpetuation of this half-truth is insufficiently catholic to avoid the serious question of there being a defect in the ministry where equality of ordination, including its accountabilities, is not taught and practiced. Both genders are helpmates in caring for and delighting in God's beloved creation, which includes God's beloved people chosen in Christ.

Notes

1. *Baptism, Eucharist and Ministry,* Faith and Order Paper No. 111 (Geneva: World Council of Churches, 1982), preface, vii. *Growth in Agreement: Reports and Agreed Statements of Ecumenical Conversations on a World Level,* ed. H. Mayer and L. Vischer (New York: Paulist Press; Geneva: World Council of Churches, 1984), 466.
2. See, for example, *Ordination Past, Present and Future: An Invitation to Dialogue,* ed. Jack Rogers and Deborah Flemister Mullen (Louisville: Presbyterian Publishing House, 1990). See also Thomas Parker, "Ordination," in *Encyclopedia of the Reformed Faith,* ed. Donald McKim (Louisville: Westminster/John Knox Press; Edinburgh: Saint Andrew Press, 1992), 263, 264; and E. David Willis, "A Reformed Doctrine of the Eucharist and Ministry and Its Implications for Roman Catholic Dialogues," *Journal of Ecumenical Studies* 21, no. 2 (Spring 1984): 295–309.
3. See the first "evangelical truth" of the Barmen Declaration in *The Book of Confessions,* Presbyterian Church (U.S.A.) (Louisville: Office of the General Assembly, 1991), 8.10.

4. John Calvin, *Institutes of the Christian Religion,* 2 vols., ed. J. T. McNeill; trans. F. L. Battles (Philadelphia: Westminster Press, 1960).
5. Ibid., 4,3,6.
6. Ibid., 4,5,4. Calvin considers pastors and teachers not to be extraordinary, temporary offices but ordinary, perpetual offices. "Next come pastors and teachers, whom the church can never go without. There is, I believe, this difference between them: teachers are not put in charge of discipline, or administering the sacraments, or warnings and exhortations, but only of Scriptural interpretation—to keep doctrine whole and pure ["healthy": *sana*] among believers. But the pastoral office includes all these functions within itself" (Ibid., 4,3,4).
7. *Baptism, Eucharist and Ministry,* Ministry II D 18, 23–24.

9

Becoming Visible:
Baptism, Women, and the Church

Although women have always been Church and today often are the
majority of active Christians, the Church is represented and becomes publicly visible as a male institution, as a long succession of
clerical men. Androcentric [i.e., male-centered] religious and liturgical language excludes women from the Divine and makes us invisible even to
our own Selves."[1] So wrote Elisabeth Schüssler Fiorenza a decade ago as
she inaugurated a new section on feminist theology for the series Concilium. Lamenting the "invisibility" and "second class citizenship" of women
in the official ministry, teaching, and liturgy of the church, Schüssler
Fiorenza went on to call for a struggle "to make women visible as God's
agents of grace and liberation."[2]

As we will see, the ecclesiastical invisibility of women scandalously
contradicts the equality accorded to them in earliest Christianity and
brought to ritual expression in baptism. The turning of the ages wrought
in Jesus Christ (Gal. 4:3–5) had its counterpart in the emergence of a community constituted not by the determinations and divisions of the old age,
but by the liberating and reconciling power of the new creation (Gal.
3:27–28; 1 Cor. 5:15–17). Baptism, as the enacted proclamation of the in-
breaking reign of God, was precisely where women became visible in a
full humanity often obscured or denied in a patriarchal world. Surely, the
baptismal liturgy today should reflect this remarkably new relation of
women and men in the church; it should, in signifying the Christian message, simultaneously make visible women's equality with men.

Toward Inclusive Worship

Before inquiring further into baptism's relation to the equal partnership
of women and men in the church, it should be noted that feminist theology has already prompted new guidelines and models for making liturgy,
including hymnody, more inclusive of women.[3] This fermenting liturgical

side of the feminist theological movement has begun to affect the officially sponsored worship resources of many denominations. This is evident, for example, in the 1989 *Directory for Worship,* 1990 *Hymnal,* and 1993 *Book of Common Worship* of the Presbyterian Church (U.S.A.).[4]

The PC(USA) directory contains a new section on the language of worship, declaring:

> The Church shall strive in its worship to use language about God which is intentionally as diverse and varied as the Bible and our theological traditions. The Church is committed to using language in such a way that all members of the community of faith may recognize themselves to be included, addressed, and equally cherished before God. Seeking to bear witness to the whole world, the Church struggles to use language which is faithful to biblical truth and which neither purposely nor inadvertently excludes people because of gender, color, or other circumstance in life.[5]

Similarly, the editorial committee of *The Presbyterian Hymnal* adopted working guidelines to assure hymns "inclusive of all God's people—sensitive to age, race, gender, physical limitations, and language," as well as a "full range of biblical images for the Persons of the Trinity."[6] Accordingly, the committee revised the wording of many, but not all, old hymns. For example, the third line of John Oxenham's "In Christ There Is No East or West," which originally read "Join hands, then, brothers of the faith, whate'er your race may be. Who serves my Father as a son is surely kin to me," now becomes "Join hands, disciples of the faith, whate'er your race may be. All children of the living God are surely kin to me." In addition, room was made for new nonsexist hymns and psalm paraphrases.

Taking its cue from the 1989 directory, the *Book of Common Worship* (1993) also signed on to the principle that "its language be inclusive, not only in reference to the people of God but also in language about God and address to God."[7] Moreover, the *Book of Common Worship* also contains an inclusive-language Psalter (a revision of that found in the 1979 Episcopal *Book of Common Prayer*) prepared by Gordon Lathrop and Gail Ramshaw. It eliminates all masculine pronouns, personal, objective, and possessive with respect to God and makes other "recurring alterations" such as replacing "brother" and "kingdom."[8]

Noting these concerns for the full inclusion of women in worship, this chapter examines the new rites of baptism, especially those prepared for American Presbyterians. I want to see how visible women are in these rites, whether that visibility can be enhanced, and how baptism can again signify the partnership of women and men in the community constituted by the new creation.

James F. Kay

Baptism and Equality in the Church

Unlike the covenantal sign of circumcision, which was exclusively reserved for males, baptism as the sign of the eternal covenant renewed in Jesus Christ is bestowed on both males and females. Baptism's gender inclusivity is indicated by the command of the risen Lord to baptize every nation (Matt. 28:19), by the New Testament accounts not only of the baptisms of males (and, on occasion, their households) but also that of Lydia and her household (Acts 16:15), and by the quotation in Galatians 3:28 from a pre-Pauline baptismal liturgy that declares, "There is no longer Jew or Greek, there is no longer slave or free, there is no longer male and female; for all of you are one in Christ Jesus."[9] As Elisabeth Schüssler Fiorenza notes, "If it was no longer circumcision but baptism which was the primary rite of initiation, then women became full members of the people of God with the same rights and duties."[10]

Schüssler Fiorenza further argues against Wayne Meeks that the formula "no longer male and female" in Galatians 3:28 does not refer to the abrogation of biological distinctions between men and women in a baptismal restoration of androgyny, but rather refers to "the first couple" (cf. Mark 10:6) and, hence, to "marriage and gender relationships." The primitive baptismal liturgy is signifying that neither patriarchal marriage nor sexual relationships between men and women constitute "the new community in Christ." Within this community, women and men are no longer "defined by their sexual procreative capacities or by their religious, cultural or social gender roles, but by their discipleship and empowering with the Spirit."[11]

Baptism, as so understood in the Pauline congregations, helps to explain why women were given such prominent roles in the first-century church. We find women as prophets (1 Cor. 11:5; Acts 21:9), deacons (Phoebe, Rom. 16:1; Dorcas, Acts 9:36), patrons (Phoebe, Rom. 16:2; Lydia, Acts 16:15; Nympha, Col. 4:15), co-workers with Paul (Euodia and Syntyche, Phil. 4:2–3), and peers in mission with their husbands (Prisca [or Priscilla] and Aquila, Acts 18:2, 18, 26; Rom. 16:3; 1 Cor. 16:19; 2 Tim. 4:19; and, "prominent among the apostles," Andronicus and Junia, Rom. 16:7). Throughout the New Testament we are afforded significant evidence that "women could enjoy a functional equality in leadership roles that would have been unusual in Greco-Roman society as a whole and quite astonishing in comparison with contemporary Judaism."[12] How the church could have so quickly abandoned the gender equality proclaimed in its baptismal liturgy, conforming its polity to the patriarchal arrangements of the Greco-Roman world, is a story that scholars are still reconstructing.[13]

Nevertheless, the very visibility of women as baptizands, from the beginnings of the church to the present, challenges their traditional invisibility in baptism as baptizers, proclaimers, and presiders, or to use the language of office, as deacons, presbyters, and bishops. Moreover, the recovery of Galatians 3:28, along with its interpretation with reference to baptism, has played a repeated role in recent years in reestablishing gender equality within the church and in reopening ordained office to women.

For example, when the World Council of Churches finally turned its full attention to the issue of women's ordination in the early 1960s, Lukas Vischer introduced the official study, *Concerning the Ordination of Women*, by asking, "Does the life of the Church adequately reflect the great truth that *in Christ there is neither male nor female?* Does the Order of the Church adequately express this truth?"[14] In this same document, Marga Bührig similarly saw Galatians 3:28 as "the place in the [New Testament] where this new relationship of men and women is most clearly formulated." By means of its teaching,

> the new category of "sister" comes into play (cf. Phil. 4:2–3, where Paul speaks in the same way of men and women as those who "have contended with him for the Gospel," see also Rom. 16:1–3). The new reality of life in the church takes woman seriously as a sister, just as it does man as brother. (It is interesting that there is no reference to maternity or motherliness. . . .) The sister remains of course a sister and does not become a brother . . . but brother and sister are on the same plane, and they come from the same "parents"—which in the case of the Christian Church means that they stand in the same relationship with God. But must this also not have consequences for their actual position in the Church, and also for their position in the world?[15]

For his part, André Dumas, citing Galatians 3:27–28, in relation to 1 Peter 2:9 and Romans 10:10, drew the consequence in his World Council of Churches discussion that "from the very outset baptism was administered to both sexes, and baptism implied being able to preach the Christian message to the world."[16]

Ironically, even though the United Presbyterian Church in the U.S.A. (UPCUSA), one of the predecessor denominations of the present Presbyterian Church (U.S.A.), began ordaining women to the ministry of Jesus Christ in 1956, the confessional basis for such action was compromised by that denomination's 1967 action bestowing constitutional status on both the Scots Confession of 1560 and the Second Helvetic Confession of 1566. Unlike the Westminster Confession of 1647, which, periodically amended, had served as the sole confession of the UPCUSA prior to 1967, both the Scots and the Second Helvetic Confession explicitly taught, in the words of the latter, "that baptism should not be administered in the church by women or midwives. For Paul deprived women of ecclesiastical duties, and baptism has to do with these."[17] Here, in protecting the visible, ecclesial character of baptism, the Confession simultaneously sanctioned the ecclesiastical invisibility of women, apparently applying Paul's silencing of Corinth's women prophets (1 Cor. 14:34) to the church practice of its own day.[18]

Faced with this confessional situation, and within a new context of feminist consciousness, "A Brief Statement of Faith," adopted by the Presbyterian Church (U.S.A.) in 1991, explicitly declares that the Holy Spirit "calls women and men to all ministries of the church."[19] In their commentary on this document, two of its drafters, William C. Placher and David Willis, list among the scriptural warrants for this declaration on ministerial calling, Galatians 3:27–29, thereby neutralizing univocal readings of 1 Corinthians 14:34.[20]

Nevertheless, Placher and Willis do join the Second Helvetic Confession in distinguishing between the "priesthood of all believers" shared by all the baptized and those "special ministries to which persons so gifted are set apart by ordination." In this way, "A Brief Statement" rejects a reading of Galatians 3:28 that, in effect, abolishes offices in the church by collapsing ordination into baptism, while simultaneously rejecting the traditional "dividing up of the ministries of the church between those to which men were called and those to which women were called." Such gender-role stereotyping results from a failure to take seriously the creation of male and female equally in the image of God and the restoration of that image wrought in Jesus Christ and proclaimed by baptism. Thus, while the Spirit does not call "*all* women and men to the ministries of the church," the Spirit does call women and men to *all* its ministries.[21]

Having seen how arguments from baptism and the baptismal liturgy found in Galatians 3:28 have supported the equal partnership of women and men in the church, we now turn to recent baptismal rites, not least to those in the Presbyterian *Book of Common Worship*. How visible are women becoming in these new rites?

The New Rites of Baptism

What follows is an examination of three elements in recent baptismal liturgies: the use of scriptural sentences serving as warrants authorizing the baptismal action, the recalling of God's covenant partners in the baptismal anamnesis, and, more controversially, the use of maternal imagery in speaking of regeneration or spiritual rebirth in the baptismal epiclesis.

Galatians 3:28 as Warrant

Despite the centrality of Galatians 3:28 in recent theological appeals for gender equality in the church, this text remains largely invisible in most of the baptismal liturgies spawned by the post–Vatican II ecumenical liturgical-renewal movement. Although Galatians 3:28 was itself a part of a first-century baptismal liturgy, it virtually disappeared from the baptismal rites of the next five centuries. Because these rites function as a norm for the liturgical-renewal movement, in that capacity they provide little precedent for reappropriating Galatians 3:28.[22] Of course, some liturgiologists would regard the notion of "scriptural warrant" as itself a quaint piece of Reformed didacticism. Nevertheless, if warrants as such are the objection, the new rites of American Lutherans, Episcopalians, Methodists, and the ecumenically drafted rite of the Consultation on Common Texts could still have woven Galatians 3:28 elsewhere in the baptismal liturgy; but not one of these rites has fully done so.[23]

In light of the liturgical invisibility of this text, it is all the more remarkable to find its appearance (with verse 27) as a warrant in the 1985 rite of Holy Baptism prepared for trial use in the Presbyterian Church (U.S.A.) and the Cumberland Presbyterian Church.[24] Beginning with this service, Galatians 3:27–28 went on to emigrate into the baptismal warrants of The Uniting Church in Australia (1988), before coming back "home" to the *Book of Common Worship* in 1993.[25]

In my judgment, the inclusion, and regular reiteration, of Galatians 3:28 at every baptism would make an incalculable contribution to the equal partnership of women and men in the church. Surely, it would not be as easy to deny ordination to women, to overlook women in the pastoral calling processes, or even to close again the once-opened door on women's ordination, as has recently taken place in the Presbyterian Church of Australia, if at every baptism it were solemnly declared that "there is no longer male and female; for all of you are one in Christ Jesus." The invisibility of women is less easy to justify where Galatians 3:28 becomes liturgically visible. In resurrecting this text, Christian baptism can once again constitute and configure the new community of equals.

Women in God's Covenant

The principal contribution of Reformed theological reflection on the sacraments lies in its reconceptualization of them as signs of the covenant. That the sacraments of Baptism and the Lord's Supper are, indeed, signs was paradigmatic for Augustine. But beginning with Zwingli in Zurich, Reformed theologians situated these sacramental signs into the broad narrative and canonical context of scripture. As a result, the primary referent of these sacramental signs became the one eternal covenant, by which is meant not a reciprocal contract between God and humanity, but God's gracious election and promise to be the God of a particular people, namely, Israel or the church. This covenant, after the Fall, was graciously renewed through Noah and his family, then through Abraham and Sarah, the exodus and the giving of the law, and the davidic kingdom, until finally renewed and confirmed in Jesus Christ.

At the time of the Reformation, the proclamation of the eternal covenant in Reformed baptismal liturgies took place either in the baptismal exhortation immediately following the scriptural warrants or in the baptismal invocation immediately before the water washing. In the recent rites inspired by the liturgical-renewal movement, preference is given to invocation over exhortation in ritually signifying the covenant and its promises. Recent rites, in giving solemn and joyful thanks for the covenant, recast the baptismal invocation into the ancient form of an anamnesis, akin to those found in the Eucharist. The 1994 Scottish *Book of Common Order* is typical in this regard:

> We thank you, gracious God,
> for your gifts of water and the Holy Spirit.
> In the beginning, you moved over the waters
> And brought light and life to a formless waste.
> By the waters of the flood,
> you cleansed the world,
> and made with Noah and his family
> a new beginning for all people.
> In the time of Moses, you led your people
> out of slavery through the waters of the sea,
> making covenant with them in a new land.
> At the appointed time,
> in the waters of the Jordan
> when Jesus was baptized by John,
> you sent your Spirit upon him.
> And now, by the baptism
> of his death and resurrection,
> Christ sets us free from sin and death
> and opens the way to eternal life.[26]

By recalling God's creation and covenant in Jesus Christ, the baptismal anamnesis serves to identify, in relation to the story of election, the God in whose Name we are commanded to baptize.

When we compare these recent baptismal invocations, we discover that the names of women are invariably absent. The Lutherans, inspired by Luther's "flood prayer," mention "Noah and his family," before recalling John who baptized God's Son. The Episcopalians name Jesus and John, and the Methodists, who also remember Noah, follow suit. The latter also speak almost clinically of Jesus as "nurtured in the water of a womb," yet fail to mention Mary by name. The rite of the Consultation on Common Texts provides two anamneses, both of which mention Noah, Jesus, and John. For their part, the Presbyterians also provide two anamneses of their own: the first mentions Noah, Jesus, and John; the second names Jesus only. Curiously, Abraham has vanished altogether, and Moses is recalled only among the Scots. But in all these rites, not one anamnesis recalls by name the role of any woman in the unfolding story of the covenant![27]

Without denying the Bible's emergence from and reflection of a patriarchal culture, can a modern baptismal rite, in recalling the biblical narrative, be less inclusive of women than the primary narrative itself? Even the Letter to the Hebrews, in summarizing the succession of the faithful in its famous eleventh chapter, manages to name Sarah, while recalling as covenantal collaborators both Rahab and "Pharaoh's daughter." The rewriting of the baptismal invocations to recall the role of women, not only as bearers of children but as bearers of God's promise, should be an urgent priority. In this way liturgy can "make women visible" for what they were—and are: "God's agents of grace and liberation."

The Womb of Regeneration

In the development of the Christian tradition, a rich mosaic of metaphors forms around baptism. According to Gabriele Winkler, the ancient Eastern liturgies contain two major interpretive patterns. The older of these, found in the Syro-Armenian rites before the end of the fourth century, is "anchored exclusively" in John 3:5 ("no one can enter the kingdom of God without being born of water and Spirit," cf. Gen. 1:2). The other pattern found in the Byzantine and later Syro-Armenian rites brings into prominence Romans 6 with its images of baptism as death and burial with Christ. Thus the Christian tradition can speak of the baptismal font as both "tomb" and "womb."[28]

In the pre–Vatican II Roman rite, the womb imagery was not predominant, but it was accented in the ritual blessing of the font at the annual Easter Vigil. According to Alex Stock, the ceremonial surrounding this blessing, such as the hand gestures dividing the water and the plunging of the paschal candle into the water, symbolized the opening of the womb and its fertilization by the grace of the Holy Spirit "so that after receiving sanctification from the immaculate womb of the divine fountain . . . a heavenly generation, born again as a new creature, may emerge."[29]

The Reformers abolished elaborate Roman rituals surrounding the blessing of the fonts, preferring to invoke God at the font that the promises given in baptism might become efficacious. Martin Bucer, for example, explicitly attacked the ancient rituals of consecrating the fonts since "no scripture teaches them, and the actual words of these prayers altogether suggest that God must impart some power immanent in these things," the same error common to the doctrine of transubstantiation. Bucer is concerned about the "magical" depersonalization of the sacraments and the resulting danger of conceiving of grace as a thing, rather than as a saving encounter with the living God.[30] Nevertheless, by suppressing the blessing of the fonts, the motif of the font as "womb," with its symbolic connection to new birth, was lost to Reformed rites.

The Vatican II liturgical reforms, influenced in part by the criticism of the Reformers, semantically altered the Roman ritual so that the blessing of the font was changed from an "actual blessing of the substance water to . . . a praising of God over the water."[31] Encouraged by this Roman reform and enamored with the ancient baptismal rites, the ecumenical liturgical-renewal movement has recovered the epiclesis or invocation of the Spirit over the font for its new rites. The *Book of Common Worship* has gone so far as to recover the term "womb" in asking the "Eternal and gracious God" to "pour out your Spirit upon us and upon this water, that this font may be your womb of new birth."[32]

While some may see this contemporary retrieval of womb imagery as congruent with scripture, ancient tradition, and the newly endorsed criterion of inclusive language, feminist liturgical theologians offer the church a caution in this regard. For example, Marjorie Proctor-Smith, acknowledging in historical baptismal rites "references to conception, gestation, and childbirth," disputes the equation of "female" with "feminist" images. Among her concerns is the danger of reinforcing "motherhood" as "the only explicitly female image found in the church's liturgical tradition," thereby becoming an "umbrella image" that either excludes women who are not mothers or suggests that motherhood should be a woman's sole vocation. In Proctor-Smith's judgment, "the emancipatory potential of the image of motherhood associated with baptism can be realized only when it is made one of several explicitly female images embodied in liturgy, when women are engaged in giving as well as receiving baptism, and when women's lived experiences of childbirth are allowed to inform the image."[33]

Here, again, Galatians 3:28 proves instructive. Baptism does not abolish the biological distinctions between women and men, but it does annul the power of procreation, whether in terms of female fecundity or male prowess, to constitute or determine the community of equals called forth by Jesus Christ. For this reason, liturgical reforms seeking to make women more visible in the church cannot be accomplished simply by retrieving a female motif here or eliminating a male pronoun there. The reform of worship according to the Word of God is not simply a matter of texts on a page, but of life in a community. Thus the liturgical abstraction or idealization of the female is no substitute for liturgy that truly leads both women and men into closer reciprocal partnership in the gospel.

In short, what is required in the proclamation and praise of the church is language that makes visible that new pattern of humanity made known in Jesus Christ, born in us by water and the Spirit, and lived out in this time and place by those women and men "on whom the end of the ages has come" (1 Cor. 10:11, RSV).

Notes

1. "Editorial," in *Women—Invisible in Theology and Church,* ed. Elisabeth Schüssler Fiorenza and Mary Collins, Concilium, vol. 182 (Edinburgh: T. & T. Clark, 1985), xi.

2. "Breaking the Silence—Becoming Visible," in ibid., 14.

3. See, among others, Ruth C. Duck, *Flames of the Spirit: Resources for Worship* (New York: Pilgrim Press, 1985), and *Finding Words for Worship: A Guide for Leaders* (Louisville: Westminster John Knox Press, 1995); Nancy A. Hardesty, *Inclusive Language in the Church* (Atlanta: John Knox Press, 1987); Rosemary Catalano Mitchell and Gail Anderson Ricciuti, *Birthings and Blessings: Liberating Worship Services for the Inclusive Church* (New York: Crossroad, 1991); Marjorie Proctor-Smith, *In Her Own Rite: Constructing Feminist Liturgical Tradition* (Nashville: Abingdon Press, 1990); Gail Ramshaw, *God Beyond Gender: Feminist Christian God-Language* (Minneapolis: Fortress Press, 1995); Rosemary Radford Ruether, *Women-Church: Theology and Practice of Feminist Liturgical Communities* (San Francisco: Harper & Row, 1985); Miriam Therese Winter, *Womanprayer, Womansong: Resources for Ritual* (Oak Park, Ill.: Meyer-Stone, 1987); and Brian Wren, *What Language Shall I Borrow? God-Talk in Worship: A Male Response to Feminist Theology* (New York: Crossroad, 1989).

4. See "Directory for Worship," in *The Constitution of the Presbyterian Church (U.S.A.), Part II, Book of Order* (Louisville: The Office of the General Assembly, 1996); *The Presbyterian Hymnal: Hymns, Psalms, and Spiritual Songs* (Louisville: Westminster/John Knox Press, 1990); and *Book of Common Worship* (Louisville: Westminster/John Knox Press, 1993).

5. "Directory for Worship," W-1. 2006b.

6. *The Presbyterian Hymnal*, 9.

7. *Book of Common Worship*, 10.

8. Ibid., 611–783. For the principles guiding this revision, see Gordon Lathrop and Gail Ramshaw, eds., *Psalter for the Christian People: An Inclusive-Language Revision of the Psalter of The Book of Common Prayer 1979* (Collegeville, Minn.: Liturgical Press, 1993), v–vii. For a critique of such principles, see Morna D. Hooker, review of *The New Testament and Psalms: An Inclusive Version*, ed. Victor Roland Gold et al., *The Princeton Seminary Bulletin*, n.s., 17 (1996): 371–73.

9. The determination that Galatians 3:28 is from a pre-Pauline baptismal liturgy is based on conclusive form-critical analysis. See in this regard Wayne A. Meeks, "The Image of the Androgyne: Some Uses of a Symbol in Earliest Christianity," *History of Religions* 13 (1974), 180–82.

10. Elisabeth Schüssler Fiorenza, *In Memory of Her: A Feminist Theological Reconstruction of Christian Origins* (New York: Crossroad, 1987), 210. From a Reformed standpoint, the language of "rights" is less satisfactory than that of "calling" or "gifts" in characterizing the ordering of responsibilities within the church.

11. Ibid., 211–13.

12. Meeks, "The Image of the Androgyne," 198.

13. See ibid., 197–208; see also Schüssler Fiorenza, *In Memory of Her*, 218–36.

14. "The Ordination of Women," in World Council of Churches, Department on Faith and Order and Department on Cooperation of Men and Women in Church, Family and Society, *Concerning the Ordination of Women*, 1964, 1. Italics original.

15. "The Question of the Ordination of Women in the Light of Some New Testament Texts," in World Council of Churches, 50.

16. "Biblical Anthropology and the Participation of Women in the Ministry of the Church," in World Council of Churches, 15–17.

17. "The Second Helvetic Confession," in *The Constitution of the Presbyterian Church (U.S.A.), Part I, The Book of Confessions* (Louisville: Office of the General Assembly, 1991), 5.191. The Confession's use of Paul to "deprive women of ecclesiastical duties" is arguably contestable by means of the Confession's own principles of scriptural interpretation. See 5.010. From "The Scots Confession," see 3.22.

18. The Confession of 1967, while explicitly condemning racial discrimination in both church and society, "did not directly address the need to correct the remaining inequalities between women and men in the church." A crisis therefore arose in 1974 after the Presbytery of Pittsburgh voted to ordain Walter Kenyon, who had stated that, if ordained, he would not participate in the ordination of women. In reversing the presbytery's action, the Permanent Judicial Commission inferred from the Confession of 1967 a constitutional prohibition of gender discrimination with respect to church office. See Jack Rogers, *Presbyterian Creeds: A Guide to the Book of Confessions* (Philadelphia: Westminster Press, 1985), 228–29.

19. "A Brief Statement of Faith," in *The Constitution of the Presbyterian Church (U.S.A.), Part I, The Book of Confessions,* 10.4, line 64.

20. William Placher and David Willis-Watkins, *Belonging to God: A Commentary on "A Brief Statement of Faith"* (Louisville: Westminster/John Knox Press, 1992), 32.

21. Ibid., 157. Cf. "The Second Helvetic Confession," 5.153.

22. In E. C. Whitaker, ed., *Documents of the Baptismal Liturgy* (London: SPCK, 1960), the use of Galatians 3:28 appears only in the Armenian rite (ninth-century manuscript). It is read as a lesson (vv. 24–29) after the filling of the font and before the invocation of the Spirit over the water.

23. See *Lutheran Book of Worship* (Minneapolis: Augsburg; Philadelphia: Lutheran Church in America, 1978), 121–25; *The Book of Common Prayer* (New York: Seabury Press, 1979), 299–314; *The United Methodist Book of Worship* (Nashville: United Methodist Publishing House, 1992), 81–114. Galatians 3:27–28 is cited by the commentary prefacing the United Methodist rite. For the rite prepared by the Consultation on Common Texts, see "An Alternative Service for the Sacrament of Baptism," *Book of Common Worship,* 419–29, where, as in the Methodist rites, the congregation welcomes the newly baptized by saying, "We are one in Christ Jesus" (429). No mention of Galatians 3:28 appears in the feminist baptismal rites proposed by Duck (*Flames of the Spirit,* 102–3), Ruether (*Women-Church,* 122–30), or Mitchell and Ricciuti (*Birthings and Blessings,* 125), but Duck subsequently endorsed its liturgical recovery. See *Gender and the Name of God: The Trinitarian Baptismal Formula* (New York: Pilgrim Press, 1991), 126.

24. *Holy Baptism and Services for the Renewal of Baptism,* Supplemental Liturgical Resource 2 (Philadelphia: Westminster Press, 1985), 22–32, esp. 25.

25. See *Uniting in Worship Leader's Book* (Melbourne: Uniting Church Press, 1988), 17–32, esp. 18; and the *Book of Common Worship,* 403–17, esp. 404.

The Australian rite drops Galatians 3:27–28 at the baptism of a child; see 35–36.

26. *Book of Common Order of the Church of Scotland* (Edinburgh: Saint Andrew Press, 1994), 88, 100–101. The *BCO* adapts here the anamnesis given in *Holy Baptism and Services for the Renewal of Baptism,* 29–30.
27. See *Lutheran Book of Worship,* 122; *Book of Common Prayer,* 306; *United Methodist Book of Worship,* 101; *Book of Common Worship,* 410–11 and 422–23 (CCT rite). Cf. Proctor-Smith, whose discussion of "feminist emancipatory baptism" calls for "evoking women's bonds and heritage by remembering the names of women in prayers and making explicit connections with women's struggles and the church's solidarity with them" (*In Her Own Rite,* 157).
28. See "The Blessing of Water in the Oriental Liturgies," in *Blessing and Power,* ed. Mary Collins and David Power (Edinburgh: T. & T. Clark, 1985), 53–61.
29. "The Blessing of the Font in the Roman Liturgy," in ibid., 43–52, citing here p. 46.
30. "Bucer's Censura," in *Christian Initiation: The Reformation Period,* ed. J. D. C. Fisher (London: SPCK, 1970), 100.
31. "The Blessing of the Font," 43.
32. *Book of Common Worship,* 411–12.
33. Proctor-Smith, *In Her Own Rite,* 158–60. Duck, in discussing classic baptismal images, ignores the new birth. See her *Gender and the Name of God,* 109–22. Ramshaw, acknowledging the difficulties of womb imagery, nevertheless appropriates it devotionally. See *Words Around the Font* (Chicago: Liturgy Training Publications, 1994), 92–96.

10

Women's Ways of Communicating: A New Blessing for Preaching

In recent years, as I have taught courses designed to provide women seminarians and women clergy with "safe spaces" in which to explore their own voices as preachers, I have been both gladdened and troubled by the stories women tell about their own preaching experiences. I have been gladdened, because I find that numerous women have fallen in love with preaching, are discovering the pulpit to be an invigorating place in which to stretch their preaching wings, and are relishing the discipline, challenge, and creativity sermon preparation affords. But I have been troubled, too, because even the best preachers seem to wrestle with demons of self-doubt. Echoing in their heads and undermining their efforts are voices telling them—either explicitly or implicitly—that their biblical insights are theologically lightweight, that they should not use so many personal examples in their sermons, or that they should keep their emotions more in check. A few women I have encountered have even become so unnerved by these demons that they literally become physically ill every time it is their turn to proclaim the gospel.

Underneath the self-doubt there seems to lie a pervasive sense, even among women who enjoy and relish the preaching task, that we women are really impostors in the pulpit; that our ways of knowing and communicating the gospel are tolerated as "experimental" (much as our theology is), but would never be blessed with the label "normative"; and that our voices, while providing a needed occasional complement to the voice of the male preacher, are still considered just that—occasional complements to normative male voices. (Witness, for example, the readiness of most larger congregations to call a woman as their associate pastor, in contrast to their unwillingness even to consider a woman as senior pastor or head of staff.)

While still in a fledgling state, research undertaken in gender, communication, and preaching suggests that one of the reasons women sometimes feel like impostors in the pulpit is that our ways of communicating are subtly, but significantly, different from those of many of our male colleagues. Women bring into the public arena of preaching patterns and modes of communication with which we have long been comfortable in the private sphere, but which may indeed seem strange to unaccustomed ears in this more public forum. Scholars refer to such traits as being "gender-linked" (rather than "gender-specific"); that is, they are communicational patterns that, because of the differences in socialization among the genders, tend to occur more commonly among women than men.

In this chapter I will explore two areas in which women's communication modes, common in the private sphere, tend to carry over into the public arena of preaching: (1) women's use of "provisional" speech (including the use of qualifiers, hedges, tag questions, and other provisional forms of syntax), and (2) women's self-disclosure in speech (focusing especially on the use of personal examples and stories in the pulpit).

Both of these are areas in which women's speech in general and preaching in particular have been criticized in the past, and there are, indeed, pitfalls associated with each of them. However, I will contend that if used with wisdom and discretion, these ways of communicating are valuable gifts women bring to the wider church and to the field of preaching in particular.

Women and the
Use of Provisional Speech

In her 1975 work *Language and Women's Place,* now a classic in the field of women's sociolinguistic research, Robin Lakoff said that women in American culture are caught in a double bind relative to their speech. If they speak as they have been trained to speak—like "ladies"—then they are considered by men to be weak, subservient, and ineffectual. If they adopt the language patterns of men, however, they are deemed to be aggressive, domineering, and pushy.

In defining what it means to speak like a "lady," Lakoff identified a number of grammatical forms she found to be more common in women's speech than in men's. For example, women use more questions than do men in conversational speech and frequently turn declarative statements into questions, either by tacking on "tag questions" (as in "It's a nice day, isn't it?") or by use of a rising intonation at the end of their sentences. Women use more qualifiers and hedges in their speech (such as "probably," "perhaps," or "it seems to me"). Women use the intensive "so" more often in their speech (as in "I like that teacher *so* much!"). Women use hypercorrect grammar (refraining from words like "ain't" and "gonna"). Women don't tell jokes.[1]

The ultimate effect of continuing to speak like a "lady," said Lakoff, is that women are systematically denied access to power on the grounds that they are deemed incapable of holding it because of their linguistic behavior. They undermine their own perceived authority by using speech men perceive to be weak and ineffectual. However, if they ignore conventional women's speech patterns, adopting the patterns of men's speech, they are seen to be overstepping their assigned place in society and are often deemed unworthy of respect. Despite the risks involved, Lakoff encourages women to become bilingual, so that they can speak not only "like a lady" but also in the mode that men deem to be more authoritative.[2]

In the twenty years since Lakoff published her work, several studies have been undertaken that have challenged, nuanced, or refined it. However, her basic description of the double bind women face is one that continues to resonate with the experience of many women. Women often feel as though they are walking a very delicate tightrope in speech—especially in those arenas where male speech has been normative. As one clergywoman said to me about her experience on a denominational committee: "If I speak up and advocate the things I believe in, I'm viewed as a 'pushy broad.' But if I'm pleasant and congenial, I get walked all over and go away feeling like I've sold my soul. It's damned if you do, damned if you don't."

But are the same risks at stake in preaching? Do women face a double bind in the pulpit as well? In her 1991 doctoral dissertation, Catherine Ziel undertook a comparative study of women's and men's preaching, asking just such questions.[3] First, are the syntactical structures Lakoff and others identify as being common to women's speech actually used with greater frequency in women's sermons than in men's?[4] And second, if they are, what is the effect upon the hearers regarding the perceived authority of the speaker? Are women seen to be less authoritative than men in the pulpit because of the speech patterns they use?

By and large, Ziel's results indicated that "women's speech" does carry over into the pulpit.[5] For example, while Ziel did not find a significant statistical difference between men and women in their use of questions in preaching, she did find that women used almost twice as many qualifiers and hedges as men used, both of the personal variety (I think, I guess, I wonder, I'm not sure) and of the more general variety (maybe, perhaps, kind of, sort of, probably). Perhaps even more significant was her observation regarding *when* women and men used hedges in preaching. Whereas women's qualifiers were rather evenly distributed throughout their sermons, men used three-fourths of their qualifiers in the first half of their sermons and only one-fourth in the second half. In other words, the closer men came to the end of their sermons, the more emphatic their speech became. Women, on the other hand, consistently tempered their speech right up until the end.

In addition, Ziel found that women tended to use more socially inclusive speech in preaching than did men (preferring "I" or "we" language to "you" language) and were also 60 percent more likely than men to use verbs of feeling or receptivity. While men used cases that related to external actions and their effects, women's sermons were peppered with phrases like "she felt" or "I hope."

On the whole, concluded Ziel, the speech of female preachers indicates that they are more likely than men to identify with their hearers in preaching and to include themselves among those addressed. They are willing to speak more explicitly about their own beliefs, thoughts, and speculations in their sermons and to emphasize the inward and personal in their speech. They are, however, less willing than men to make unqualified statements and, for whatever reasons, prefer greater ambiguity and qualification in their proclamation.

But does women's speech in the pulpit place clergywomen in the same double bind that Lakoff spoke of? Are female clergy perceived to be less authoritative than their male colleagues when they use the speech patterns with which they are most comfortable?

In order to test perceptions, Ziel wrote a sermon and cast it in two forms, one using male speech and one using female speech. She then made two audio tapes of the sermon preached in each speech mode, one with a male preaching and the other with a female preaching (in order to preclude judgment on the basis of gender alone). She asked groups of congregants to listen to each sermon, evaluating it in relation to pairs of nineteen adjectives related to the perceived authority of the preacher. Because of her own belief that women were operating out of a different understanding of authority than were men, she included pairs of adjectives related to traditional understanding of authority (such as, "Did you perceive the preacher to be logical or confused? Did you perceive the preacher to be powerful or weak?") as well as those related to a more relational understanding of authority ("Did you perceive the preacher to be more concerned about people or about ideas? Did you perceive the preacher to be more flexible or more rigid?"). Her expectation was that the sermons written in male syntax would be perceived as more logical, powerful, confidant, decisive, forceful, and bold than sermons written in female syntax.

The test results as a whole, however, did not support this hypothesis. In fact, when taken as a group, there was little difference in perception of authority—however it was defined—on the part of the hearers. But when Ziel analyzed the test results more closely, she observed an interesting phenomenon. The one juncture at which there was significant difference between women's and men's authority ratings occurred with the sermons that used female syntax. Women consistently rated sermons using women's speech—whether preached by a woman or a man—above the mean, whereas men consistently rated them lower. In other words, women consistently found sermons preached in women's syntax to be more authoritative than did men.

How then, do we judge the potential of women's speech in the pulpit? Is it an asset or a liability, a double bind or a blessing?

Certainly women's speech, like any speech, needs to be checked against misuse or excesses, whether it is employed by women or by men. I have witnessed beginning students in preaching class of both genders, though most frequently women, who precede every new sermonic idea with an "I think" or "It seems to me." The effect on the hearers is that the preacher *does* sound either apologetic or uncertain.

On the other hand, the use of qualifiers, hedges, and other characteristics of women's speech can also serve very positive purposes in a sermon. Witness, for example, Barbara Brown Taylor's use of these devices in a section of her sermon titled "The Fourth Watch." She has just finished retelling the story from Mark 6 (vv. 48–50) about Jesus coming to the disciples at night while they are in a boat in strong winds, the disciples mistaking Jesus for a ghost, Jesus climbing into the boat and calming the winds, and the disciples still missing the point. She continues:

> Now for me, at least, this is not a satisfying story. I prefer a little more bravado in my disciples, or at least the assurance that they have learned their lesson. But according to Mark, they just did not get it. They did not recognize that their rabbi was also the Messiah they had been waiting for, and it was not very satisfying for Mark either. The only explanation he could think of was that their hearts were hardened—their minds were closed—so that they did not understand the miracle of the loaves or much of anything else for that matter.
>
> Maybe that explains why they were not glad to see Jesus. . . .

(And Taylor proceeds to describe the disciples' brand of hardening of the heart—or "cardiosclerosis" as she calls it—and Jesus' gracious response of getting into the boat with them, opening his own heart to them, and telling them to "take heart.")[6]

Note how Taylor uses women's syntax several times, but in each instance the effect is not to make her speech sound apologetic. Rather, in each case her syntax serves a positive rhetorical function.

For example, she begins her response to this story with a hedge or qualifier: "Now for me, at least, this is not a satisfying story." And she follows it with speech explicitly stating her own point of view: "I prefer a little more bravado in my disciples. . . ." The effect? Through her "women's way of speaking," Taylor invites the hearers to join her in being frustrated with the disciples' response to Jesus. By admitting her own dissatisfaction with their response, she opens the way in a highly invitational manner for others to admit their own.

Her second qualified phrase, "Maybe that explains why they were not glad to see Jesus . . ." is equally invitational. Without forcing the hearers to accept her interpretation of the text, she posits it and invites their consideration of it. In the sentences that follow, she states her own point of view clearly and without apology. But her use of a qualifier also grants the hearers space and freedom to ponder her point of view and to decide for themselves whether or not they agree with her.

In her book *Gendered Lives,* Julia T. Wood, professor of communication at the University of North Carolina, notes that a number of scholars researching women's speech since Robin Lakoff have challenged Lakoff's contention that women's speech always reflects women's socialization into subordinate roles and low self-esteem. Wood says:

> Rather than reflecting powerlessness, the use of hedges, qualifiers, and tag questions may express women's desires to keep conversation open and to include others. It is much easier to jump into a conversation that has not been sealed with absolute, firm statements. A tentative style of speaking supports women's general desire to create equality and include others. It is important to realize, however, that people outside of women's speech community may misinterpret women's intentions in using tentative communication.[7]

Ziel's finding that men considered the sermons preached using women's syntax less authoritative than did women underscores Wood's recognition that women risk misinterpretation when they use such speech. However, the fact that women consistently rated such speech as being more authoritative should not be undervalued.

Wood's observations bring to mind the response I recently heard a female parishioner give to a sermon preached by a visiting clergywoman. "At last," she exclaimed in delight, "a sermon I didn't have to constantly translate into my own categories!" Women's speech, when wisely modeled in the pulpit, allows countless women (as well as men who have an affinity for such speech) to hear the gospel in a communicational mode that does not require of them constant translation. And for many of them, such a hearing is long overdue.

Furthermore, Wood's identification of some of the positive attributes of tag questions, qualifiers, and hedges suggests that risks in misinterpretation are worth taking for the sake of the values gained. There is something highly appropriate—not only communicationally but also theologically—about using speech that creates equality, includes others, and invites rather than demands a response—especially when preaching a gospel that does the same. At first, such speech may sound less "authoritative" (as traditionally defined) to unaccustomed ears. But in the final analysis, persuasion by free consent, as opposed to persuasion by coercion, is far preferable.

In addition to its invitational tone, women's speech—with its preference for "we" language (as opposed to "you" language) and with its strong ability to create an environment in which the preacher converses *with* the congregation *about* a text, as Taylor does when she discusses with the congregation her own dislike for the disciples' response in this story—brings other valuable gifts to the pulpit. Walter Brueggemann observes that one of the problems with contemporary preaching is that all too often in the triangle created between preacher, text, and congregation (to borrow a family-systems analogue), preacher and text team up to "triangle" against the hearers.[8] The preacher speaks as if his or her word and the text's word are identical, and thus gives the congregation no room for talking back. The congregation, predictably, becomes hostile at being made the odd one out in the triangle. Far better, says Brueggemann, if both preacher and hearers stand together before the text, hearing together its scandalous word of grace and of judgment.

Finally, women's speech, through its modeling of a different style of exercising authority in the pulpit, pushes the church to reconsider its traditional understanding of this term. Christine Smith, author of the first feminist textbook on preaching, writes:

> Authority in preaching has traditionally been defined as that quality of proclamation that pertains to special rights, power, knowledge, and capacity to influence or transform. . . . From a feminist perspective . . . preaching is not so much a matter of the right and privilege of the position with all its distinctive power; rather it is a craft of authenticity weaving together mutuality, solidarity, and deeper faith sharing. Therefore, authority and intimacy are of necessity inextricably woven together in feminist preaching.[9]

In women's speech, authority and intimacy are indeed inextricably woven together as the preacher creates from the pulpit an environment that invites connectedness with the hearers and encourages interdependence in discerning the gospel's claims for life. Such a model, as theologian Letty Russell reminds us, challenges traditional understandings of authority and urges us to consider a new paradigm for authority—authority as "partnership" exercised in Christ's "household of freedom."[10]

Women's Self-Disclosure in the Pulpit

During the 1980s, two professors of preaching, Edwina Hunter and Christine Smith, interviewed a number of their colleagues regarding the differences observed between male and female preachers in their classrooms.[11] Most of the responses they received focused on the tendency of women to be more self-disclosive in the pulpit than men.

For example, in a survey undertaken by Hunter, almost all the teachers interviewed said that women used personal examples more often and more freely than did men. Several commented on women's ability to "concretize" and "get right to the heart of the issues" found in the biblical text. Others noted that women frequently used metaphors and images that arose out of their own experience, including their experience of oppression.

When Smith conducted her interviews several years later, similar themes emerged. A male professor at a nondenominational seminary said of the women in his classes:

> Women use more images and more stories. Men use more exegetical development. The [biblical] texts women choose are less abstract and more related to everyday, real-life issues. . . . Women are almost always more self-revealing than men, and more consistently begin with the contemporary experience and move to the text rather than moving from text to experience.[12]

A female professor at a Methodist seminary said, "Women have a greater awareness of the interconnectedness of the personal level to the social justice level. Women are much more communal and have higher degrees of self-disclosure."[13]

Smith followed her interviews with a study of four collections of women's sermons and once again found parallel trends.[14] She discovered, for instance, that in all four sermon collections the use of story, especially stores women had actually lived, was pervasive. She also observed that the sermons by women were "rich in imagery, poetic language, and personal illustrations from women's lives," and that themes of oppression, suffering, and pain were recurrent.[15]

But is this tendency toward greater self-disclosure a strength women bring to the pulpit, or is it a liability? Is it bane or blessing for the homiletical task?

Certainly, if used wisely and well, there are tremendous benefits congregations can gain from women's propensity toward personal storytelling in the pulpit. For starters, self-disclosive speech has a highly relational quality to it, as the preacher allows the hearers a glimpse into her own life-world and seeks to establish some common bond with the hearer through the telling of a particular story with more universal applications. Witness Susan Auchincloss, a pastor in Prague, in the Czech Republic, forging such linkages through a story that occurs near the beginning of her sermon on repentance:

> I remember once when my grandparents were visiting us—they always did over the Christmas holidays, since my mother was an only child. It was a Sunday morning and we were going to church. My grandmother couldn't bear to be on time for church; she had to be early. If she couldn't sit in the front near the center, she scarcely cared if she went to church or not. So she would corral us children and make sure we were reading and waiting in the car with her. We, at least, wouldn't cause any delay. That Sunday I followed her out of the house, down the flagstone steps through the garden, almost to the car and then I said, trying to hide my glee—for even children enjoy it when the mighty are fallen—"Mimi, you forgot your skirt!" She peered with difficulty over the elegant, hand-knitted suit jacket, which covered an ample bosom, but sure enough, there she stood in her slip. Needless to say, she turned on the spot and went to set herself right.

I tell that story because I want to talk about repentance. Repentance translates the Greek word, *metanoia,* which means literally, a mental turnaround. But it is much more than a change of mind or even a change of mind and heart. The whole being makes a 180 degree turn in *metanoia*—heart, mind, will, body, spirit, soul—and all together like a pond turning over in the spring.[16]

Through this story taken from her own experience, Auchincloss not only gives us a glimpse into her family life as a child, where church attendance was an assumed part of life, where grandmother came to visit every Christmas, and where grandchildren delighted in getting the best of their elders. She also invites us to recollect similar experiences: of grandmothers with set behaviors or ample bosoms or both, of the glee that comes from seeing an overly rigid person do something totally embarrassing, and of a simpler time when families all piled into cars and headed off to church as if it were the most ordinary thing in the world to do on Sunday morning.

In her best-selling book about women's and men's conversational styles, titled *You Just Don't Understand,* Deborah Tannen says that women tend to favor "rapport-talk" in their speech, while men favor "report-talk." That is, women use conversations as a means of establishing connections and negotiating relationships, while men use conversation as a means for preserving independence and negotiating status in a hierarchical social order. Women place emphasis on displaying similarities and matching experiences with their conversation partners; men place emphasis on exhibiting knowledge and skill, or holding center stage through their storytelling, joking, or imparting of information.[17]

We can easily imagine, as we hear the story Auchincloss tells in her sermon, that men or women or children might want to stop on their way out of church or pause during a cup of coffee in the fellowship hall to chuckle anew at the scene she paints or to share a similar story of their own. The story not only gives the hearers a sense of knowing more about their pastor. Like leaven in a loaf, it also itself provides an invitation, a catalyst for such relationship-building conversations to continue.

But Auchincloss does more than elicit our common memories or build rapport through the telling of this story. Through it she also provides us with an image—a visual, down-to-earth, and feminine (though not stereotypical) image—of *metanoia,* repentance. What is *metanoia* like? It is like suddenly realizing that your slip is showing all over the place, that you are not dressed as you would like to be, and that in order to become reclothed, you need to turn your whole self around and make haste to change. Indeed, toward the conclusion of her sermon Auchincloss returns to the tale of her grandmother, this time positing her not as "fool" (who forgets her skirt), but as "wise woman" whose immediacy in turning is to be emulated by the hearers.

Smith says that one of the reasons women tell personal stories from the pulpit is that through their stories women are able to name reality from a woman's perspective. "Naming," says Smith, "is a critical feminist issue. Women have relied on oral tradition throughout time as a means of preserving their 'herstory' and remembering their identities as women."[18] Through their sermons, then, women continue the important task of naming the world and God's presence in it through the lens of their own feminine experiences. Through her sermon, Auchincloss renames a classical theological concept "repentance" in a new and markedly feminine way.

Yet there is still another reason that women tend toward self-disclosure in the pulpit, and it has to do with a "connected" mode of knowing common among women. In their book *Women's Ways of Knowing,* Mary Field Belenky and her colleagues distinguish between "separate" and "connected" modes of knowing.[19] *Separate* knowing is the kind of understanding women acquire through higher education. In separate knowing, the goal is to keep the learning mode as objective, dispassionate, and analytical as possible. The starting point for the separate knower is a suspicion of the opinion of another. Thus, in order to be persuasive, the owner of the opinion must defend it in as rational and nonsubjective a mode as possible.

In *connected* knowing, on the other hand, the subjective is highly valued. The would-be knower begins from a stance of empathy and seeks to understand not only the position of the other, but also why the other holds such a position. So, for example, a connected knower would want to know not only what a poet wrote, but also what was going on in the poet's life at the time that caused him or her to write such a poem. Similarly, learning is not complete for the connected knower until the knower has discerned the significance of the knowledge for his or her own life and understanding. To follow the poetry analogy, the connected knower does not just want to know what the poem means. The connected knower asks, "What does this poem mean to me?"[20]

Because of their connected modes of knowing, many women tend to use personal experience and examples, rather than more abstract modes of argumentation, when explaining ideas, not only in private conversations but also in the pulpit. In so doing they are espousing a form of logic that not only makes perfect sense to them rationally but also existentially.

However, studies indicate that such patterns of communication may indeed hold liabilities for women—especially in their communication with men. For example, one study of faculty meetings in a secondary school in England found that women's arguments did not carry as much weight with their male colleagues when women introduced their own experience as evidence or when they argued policy decisions on the basis of their potential effects on particular students. The men preferred arguments that used categorical statements related to right and wrong.[21] Tannen says that when women bring their own experience into arguments, men sometimes perceive them as being "irrational" rather than recognizing that they are operating according to a different system of logic.

And in homiletics itself, the use of personal examples is still highly suspect in some quarters. Witness David Buttrick's words in *Homiletic:*

> To be blunt, there are virtually no good reasons to talk about ourselves from the pulpit. . . . Research indicates that (1) congregations—even when prompted by "Has something like that happened to you?"—will *never* bring to mind similar experiences from their own recall, and (2) congregations will *always* remember the illustration as a disclosure of the *preacher's* character. . . . The illustration will not illumine the idea intended.[22]

Certainly there are pitfalls to be avoided when taking personal examples or stories into the pulpit. Thomas G. Long provides a good checklist for the preacher: "Don't always make yourself the hero; don't reveal pastoral confidences; don't embarrass a child or a spouse; don't turn the pulpit into a confessional; do tell experiences with which the hearers can identify."[23] But should we say that there is never any good reason to talk about ourselves from the pulpit? Not only am I unpersuaded by the premises on which Buttrick makes this assertion; I also see many positive values that this "connected" style of preaching brings to the pulpit.

Through the telling of their own stories, women model for the community of faith how to find, in the ordinary, mundane experiences of everyday life, inbreakings of the holy. Through the telling of their own stories, women keep the gospel close to the ground, making very local connections between the biblical story and our lived lives. Through the telling of their own stories, women provide an accessible model through which children and less educated folk in a congregation can find their own voices and give expression to their own faith and understanding. Through the telling of their own authentic stories, women provide a needed corrective to a pulpit too long held hostage by sports stories, war stories, and canned illustrations of every variety.

Conclusion

Yes, there are liabilities with women's self-disclosure in the pulpit, just as there are liabilities with women's syntax. But there are also benefits—valuable benefits—that women bring to the pulpit through their distinctive ways of communicating the gospel. Perhaps, then, the appropriate response to the double bind women face in the pulpit is not that women continually adapt to "normative" male communicational modes. Rather, in a partnership of equals, both women and men bring their "best selves" to the pulpit, learning from one another new ways of knowing and speaking the faith.

Notes

1. Robin Lakoff, *Language and Women's Place* (New York: Harper & Row, 1975). For a summary of the speech forms Lakoff identifies as comprising "women's language," see pp. 53–57.

2. Ibid., 74–75, 83.

3. For her study, Ziel solicited three tape-recorded sermons from each of sixteen preachers—eight women and eight men. In order to exercise some controls, all were ordained ministers of the Evangelical Lutheran Church in America, serving as sole pastors of congregations between two hundred and one thousand members in the Northeastern Pennsylvania Synod. All of them had no less than two and no more than ten years' experience in parish ministry. See Catherine A. Ziel, "Mother Tongue/Father Tongue: Gender-Linked Differences in Language Use and Their Influence on the Perceived Authority of the Preacher" (Ph.D. diss., Princeton Theological Seminary, 1991).

4. Ziel tested the sermons for the frequency of six gender-linked traits: (1) tag questions; (2) other questions; (3) qualifiers and hedges; (4) socially inclusive language ("we" versus "you"); (5) use of explicit participative cases (dealing with internal states such as thinking and feeling); and (6) use of instrumental cases. See ibid., 29–30.

5. For a summary and analysis of Ziel's statistical findings, see ibid., 118–64.

6. Barbara Brown Taylor, "The Fourth Watch," a sermon in *The Preaching Life* (Boston: Cowley Publications, 1993), 96.

7. Julia T. Wood, *Gendered Lives: Communication, Gender, and Culture* (Belmont, Calif.: Wadsworth Publishing Co., 1994).

8. Walter Brueggemann, "The Preacher, Text, and People," *Theology Today* 47 (October 1990): 239–47.

9. Christine M. Smith, *Weaving the Sermon: Preaching in a Feminist Perspective* (Louisville: Westminster/John Knox Press, 1989), 46–47.

10. Letty M. Russell, *Household of Freedom: Authority in Feminist Theology* (Philadelphia: Westminster Press, 1987). See esp. chap. 2, "Paradigms of Authority," 30–41.

11. In 1984, Hunter (then on the faculty of the Pacific School of Religion) interviewed thirteen professors (one woman, two black men, and ten white men) in ten seminaries. An interpretive summary of her findings can be found in "Weaving Life's Experiences into Women's Preaching," *The Christian Ministry* (September-October 1987): 14–17.

    Several years later, Christine Smith (then on the faculty of Princeton Theological Seminary) conducted a written survey of ten professors of homiletics (eight men and two women), representing a geographical cross section of the country and a wide range of denominations. A summary of her findings can be found in *Weaving the Sermon,* 11–13.

12. Smith, *Weaving the Sermon,* 12–13.

13. Ibid., 13.

14. The four collections Smith studied were as follows: Helen Gray Crotwell, ed., *Women and the Word: Sermons* (Philadelphia: Fortress Press, 1978);

idem., *Spinning a Sacred Yarn: Women Speak from the Pulpit* (New York: Pilgrim Press, 1982); Ella Pearson Mitchell, ed., *Those Preachin' Women: Sermons by Black Women Preachers* (Valley Forge, Pa.: Judson Press, 1985); Charles D. Hackett, ed., *Women of the Word: Contemporary Sermons by Women Clergy* (Marietta, Ga.: Cherokee Publishing Co., 1985).

15. Smith, *Weaving the Sermon,* 14–15.
16. Susan Auchincloss, "Repent, *Metanoeite,*" in *Best Sermons 5,* ed. James W. Cox (San Francisco: HarperCollins, 1992), 39.
17. Deborah Tannen, *You Just Don't Understand: Women and Men in Conversation* (New York: Ballantine Books, 1990), 77.
18. Smith, *Weaving the Sermon,* 14.
19. Mary Field Belenky, Blythe McVicker Clinchy, Nancy Rule Goldberger, and Jill Mattuck Tarule, *Women's Ways of Knowing: The Development of Self, Voice and Mind* (New York: Basic Books, 1986), 100–130.
20. Ibid.
21. Celia Roberts and Tom Jupp presented the findings of this study at the 1985 Linguistics Institute, Georgetown University. Deborah Tannen cites it in *You Just Don't Understand,* 91–92.
22. David Buttrick, *Homiletic: Moves and Structures* (Philadelphia: Fortress Press, 1987), 142.
23. Thomas G. Long, *The Witness of Preaching* (Louisville: Westminster/John Knox Press, 1989), 177.

11

Gender and
Small Group Communication in the Church

A church is not a static entity. As we know all too well, a church that was healthy and vital twelve months ago may be in trouble today. The good news, however, is that a church that is struggling for its very life this week may be a vibrant, Spirit-filled Christian community next year. Things change. That is a given. What is not a given is whether that change will be for the better or for the worse.

Because of the constancy of change, the church is in a continual process of creating itself anew. Stalwart leaders of the church die. Families active in community life move to another city, and new folks with different interests and needs start coming to church. Change is not dependent on losing or adding members, however. If a group within the church dedicates itself to a special year of study and prayer for the world, its members may mature in their Christian life in ways that will deeply enrich their whole community. It may not be obvious to anyone but the most careful observer how the community is being influenced as a result of changes occurring among members in the prayer group. Yet, over time, the church may experience significant renewal, due in large part to changes that were initiated in the lives of a small group of faithful Christians.

The aspect of change and church renewal on which I will focus involves encouraging strong and healthy working relationships among women and men in the church. If we are committed to encouraging leadership by women and men in the church, we must continually review this commitment and evaluate whether or not it is being energized by effective thought and action. Researchers have found that groups committed to egalitarian relationships among women and men fall back into old communication patterns that undermine their commitment; but when groups remind themselves periodically of their commitment and review their communication, they are able to sustain healthier, more egalitarian patterns of communication.[1]

Fortunately, the dynamic process that constitutes and renews the church is not the result of human effort alone. The most important element in the process is the work of the Holy Spirit. If the church community is to be healthy, we must seek to discern and cooperate with the work of the Spirit in everything we do. The grace of God can creatively transform a stagnant community, even when human eyes can see no way out of the morass. Faith in God, who both transcends the reality of our world and yet is intimately engaged in every moment of our existence, gives us reason for hope. Faith in God's role in the process can give us the courage and strength to address our responsibility for the human elements that constitute the social reality we call the church.

We each perceive the church based on our participation in the communication events that constitute the social reality of the church.[2] When we think of communication events that constitute church life, we think first of worship. The reading of scripture, preaching, prayer, the children's sermon, and music are some of the communication events that create a worship service. It is beyond the scope of this chapter to develop the many ways in which elements of worship influence how women and men understand themselves in relationship to the church. However, let me mention briefly a few elements that deserve our consideration.

How do people who speak during the service refer to women and men? Are females subsumed within references to "man," and "mankind," and "he"? Although the word "man" has been used for centuries as if it were generic, women and men furrow their brows when they hear "the sisterhood of man." If *man* truly functioned as a generic term that includes women, this phrase should work, but our ears tell us that it does not. Children, even as old as junior-high age, often interpret *man* and *mankind* as referring only to men.[3] This has implications for how boys and girls interpret what they hear in church. By using *human beings* or *women and men,* we can be sure everyone is included.

Other elements of worship also influence how women and men will understand themselves in relationship to the church. Are all the visible church leaders during worship men? Do illustrations in sermons refer to women and men only in stereotypic social roles? Do exegetical treatments of scripture ever focus on the positive roles of women in Bible stories? Are the feminine metaphors for God found in the Bible ever emphasized? Is there art in the sanctuary? If so, how are women and men depicted? What messages about men and women are found in the music?

Through verbal and nonverbal processes, worship services are filled with messages about women and men and their place in the church. A church that is committed to encouraging each person to develop and use his or her God-given talents to the fullest needs to ask what messages people are receiving about women and men when they attend worship.

Although worship is central to the life and identity of the church, it is not the only important site of communication events that create and sustain Christian community. In the six days and twenty-some hours each week when we are not in a worship service together, thousands of intentional and unintentional, verbal and nonverbal communication events occur that also help create the community, including the perceptions women and men have about their value and place in it. Much of this communication occurs in small groups; for example, the church session, the education committee, church staff meetings, the new member committee, a Bible-study group, prayer group, or an informal group that gathers for lunch following church.[4]

Churches are also becoming more interested in support groups, a type of group to which 40 percent of the people in the United States belong.[5] Many churches hope that tapping into this interest in our society will contribute to church renewal. It is important to realize, though, that all small groups, not just support groups, provide opportunities for enriching and renewing the life of the church.

While it is true that groups play an influential role in church life, the role they play is not necessarily positive. That which can do great good can also do great harm. One can use the flame of a candle to read the Bible or burn down a church. We should not be afraid of small groups, but we should not be naive about them either. Many of the painful stories women report about the church occurred in a small group in which they were treated in a demeaning and insulting way by a dominant male. Often other group members are appalled at the behavior but are unprepared to stop it. Their silence can leave a woman feeling isolated and abused.

Recently, one of my students at Princeton Theological Seminary shared a disturbing story of her experience with a search committee. An older professional male who opposed hiring women, particularly as senior pastor, attempted to intimidate her during a group interview by asking questions in an aggressive tone of voice and telling her that her questions were totally inappropriate. The younger male and female members of the committee looked uncomfortable but did nothing. The candidate, a mature, professional woman with many years of experience, was able to hold her own, but the pain caused by the unexpected treatment reverberated within her for weeks. Fortunately, the woman was an excellent candidate and was eagerly pursued to become the first female senior pastor of another large church where she has been warmly welcomed by men and women alike.

Unfortunately, her story about the search committee is not an isolated one. Not only are female candidates hurt when subjected to such abusive behavior, but so are the other members of the committee. The women who were on the search committee continue to be part of that church. What do they now think of the way women are viewed in their church?

Of course, we cannot always stop people from behaving destructively. However, we need to anticipate possible destructive behavior and be prepared to intervene if it occurs. The man on the search committee had been elected to serve. However, his propensity to try to intimidate women in church groups was known by church leaders. Other members of the search committee should have been prepared to insist that he follow the guidelines for conducting interviews.

One of the biggest challenges in creating healthy small groups is appropriate identification and training of leaders. If anyone is allowed to lead a group, without any guidance or process of accountability, the person may use the role of leader destructively. If people have negative experiences in groups, those experiences will influence their perception of the church as a whole. It is critical, then, to think about specific ways the values and commitments of the church are embodied or undermined in groups. Understanding more about how communication works and about gender differences in communication can help us with this process.

Insights from Communication
Research and Theory

A first important principle of communication is: You cannot *not* communicate.[6] Consider the following situation. Doug is the leader of a Bible-study group that is focusing on the life of Moses. Although he's been very busy, he spent lots of time preparing material about Moses' relationship with Aaron. When he begins the study with open-ended questions, Marsha points out how significant women were in Moses' life. Doug keeps trying to direct the discussion toward Moses' relationship with Aaron, but somehow Moses' sister, Miriam, and Pharaoh's daughter keep getting all of the attention.

Finally Doug decides to just quit trying. He's tired. The group does not seem interested in the material he prepared, and they are having a fruitful and energetic discussion. He begins to jot down a few notes for an important meeting tomorrow.

After the meeting Marsha tells Doug she is upset about the way he responded to the discussion of the women in Moses' life. Doug is genuinely surprised. He didn't think he was being negative. He was prepared to discuss Aaron, and not the women, so he had nothing to add to the discussion. Marsha is unconvinced.

"I wasn't communicating anything!" Doug repeated. "I was just sitting there. I was perfectly happy for the discussion to go in the direction it did!"

Two questions arise:

1. Doug claims not to have communicated anything. What details led Marsha to think that Doug was being negative?
2. Has anyone ever interpreted your behavior as significant when you were unaware that you were communicating anything at all?

Gender and Small Group Communication

Communication is a complex process. We communicate many messages to people every day without being aware of it. Whenever we are in someone's presence, that person may attribute meaning to our behavior. If I pass a colleague in the hall who thinks I saw him and didn't speak, he's likely to attribute meaning to my behavior. If he's offended, I will be fortunate if he tells me, and I have a chance to explain. Maybe I lost my contact lenses and had no idea anyone was in the hall!

These examples are hardly momentous. Yet such communication helps create the emotional tone of a community. If I regularly walk through the church not acknowledging anyone, if I ignore people in groups when they talk about things I'm not interested in, and if I draw distractedly, I may offend or discourage others. As the first principle of communication states, you cannot *not* communicate.

Often the messages we send that offend others are nonverbal. A second principle of communication clarifies the function of nonverbal communication. Every message contains both a content (verbal) and a relationship (nonverbal) dimension. The relationship (nonverbal) dimension of a message frames the content (verbal) dimension of the message and determines how we interpret it. Consider the statement, "This group better come to order." What kind of statement is it? Depending on how it is spoken, it may be a joke, a threat, or a statement of resignation. Tone of voice, rate of speech, inflection, facial expression, posture, gestures, touch, time, and use of space are all nonverbal elements that help us interpret the content of a message.

The challenge of correctly interpreting nonverbal behavior increases when people are from different cultures. If a couple from Japan joins a Bible-study group, their English may be flawless, yet the differences in nonverbal behavior may create misunderstandings. People in Japan value the ability to maintain a serene face in public. They show respect by avoiding direct eye contact. If the Japanese couple uses minimal facial expressiveness and tends not to look others in the eye, other group members may think they are unfriendly and intentionally enigmatic. Such negative attributions commonly occur when we are unaware of the cultural, racial, and ethnic differences in nonverbal communication.

The nonverbal dimension of a message creates and reflects the nature of our relationship with others. One aspect of relationship we negotiate in every communication event is control and power.[7] Who will speak first? Who can talk about what? Whose office will we meet in? As we negotiate these issues, our nonverbal behavior signals whether we perceive others as equal, superior, or inferior to us. We may say with our words that another is our equal, but if our nonverbal behavior contradicts our words, people usually believe the nonverbal.

In the United States, certain nonverbal behaviors are associated with people in authority. In a group, they tend to look at others less than others look at them. When speaking, they tend to look at everyone in the group, whereas others will tend to address their comments to the person with authority. Persons with authority usually take up more space at the table and sit more informally. They may initiate touch, such as a congratulatory slap on the back, but those with less power are unlikely to touch them. Persons with authority have more influence than others over who talks, about what topics, and for what length of time. In organizations with clear lines of authority, one can see the power differences by observing nonverbal behavior.

One of the complicating factors in male-female communication is that the differences in nonverbal behavior between white, middle-class men and women in the United States parallel the differences between people with greater and lesser degrees of authority. Women tend to look at other speakers more than men do, take up less space, sit more formally, and touch men less than men touch them. Because of these gender differences, men communicate authority and power more than women do. Unless we are conscious of the nonverbal dynamics involved in negotiating power, it can be difficult to establish egalitarian relationships.

Another way power is expressed in small groups is in the total amount of time a person speaks. Although one commonly hears that women talk more than men, research finds the opposite to be true. Linguists Deborah James and Janice Drakich reviewed fifty-six studies of mixed-sex interactions among middle-class English-speaking Americans done between 1951 and 1991.[8] In twenty-four of the studies (42 percent), males talked more than females. In another ten studies (17.9 percent), males talked more than females in some circumstances, and an equal amount in others. In four studies (7.1 percent), researchers found that men talked more sometimes, and women talked more sometimes. In sixteen studies (28.6 percent), no difference was found. Women talked more than men overall in only two of the fifty-six studies (3.6 percent).

Given these data, why does the stereotype of the talkative woman persist? One explanation is that women talk more to one another privately than men do. Men talk more publicly.[9] Another explanation points to the historical ideal of the silent woman in terms of which any amount of talk by a woman is too much.[10] Kathleen Hall Jamieson, dean of the Annenberg School for Communication at the University of Pennsylvania, reminds us that in seventeenth-century America, a woman who spoke out in public could expect to be bound to a ducking stool and submerged under water. When she was brought up, gasping for air, she was offered the choice between silence and drowning. If she repented and promised to be silent, her life would be spared. The lesson was not lost on other women. It was not wise to speak in ways that men thought disrupted the social order.[11] Jamieson reviews the history of restricting women from public speaking, restrictions that continue today in churches that forbid women to preach. This history helps explain why women report more difficulty in gaining a hearing for their ideas in public and having their ideas respected, and why they are less likely to speak on controversial topics. It may also help explain why "boys speak more in class, are more likely to be called on by teachers, and are less frequently reprimanded than girls for not raising their hands to speak and being 'impolite.'"[12] As we think of the implications of this research for women and men in the church, we need to pay attention to how boys and girls are learning to relate in our Sunday school classes and in youth groups.

If women and men are to work together effectively, it is important that women not be restricted from full participation in the group process. Because males use nonverbal behaviors associated with those in power, and talk more in most groups, women may not feel they are treated as equals in a group. If women in a group experience the men as controlling, but the men genuinely want to relate to women as equals, it would be helpful to videotape the group to study the nonverbal behavior and the amount of time each person talks. We can learn a great deal by observing ourselves in action.

You may begin to worry that if we study our communication behavior carefully, we will be able to use our knowledge to manipulate others. It's a valid concern. The more we understand about communication, the more we can contribute to the health of our church. At the same time, the more we understand about the communication process, the more damage we can do. As we know all too well, those who have skillfully manipulated others for their own purposes, while claiming to be representatives of God, have perpetrated some of the most heinous evil the world has ever known. The answer, though, is not to avoid learning more about communication. Rather, as a healthy Christian community, we need to find helpful ways to hold ourselves, and one another, accountable for communicating ethically.

How do we account for differences in the ways women and men communicate? Two theories have been advanced that are part of a lively debate currently being carried on in the halls of academia and in books on the best-seller list.

Dominance Theory

The first theory emphasizes power differences that exist between women and men.[13] Differences in economic and political power translate into men being valued more than women. Egalitarian relationships may be possible, but they are hard to create and sustain. Centuries of sex discrimination created patterns of male domination and female submission that influence all of us. It is as if we were trying to redirect a great surging river. Until new river beds are firmly established, the river will return to its old ways.

Janet L. Weathers

Unless we are alert, we can fall back into destructive patterns. Where sexism is present in a community, men speak more than do women, regardless of their respective levels of expertise. Men are assumed to be more competent than women in everything except those roles specifically designated as women's work. Sexism influences the ways we think about others and the ways we think about ourselves. Women and men often evaluate messages sent by men as more effective, more organized, and more persuasive than messages sent by women, even when the messages are identical. It is just such prejudicial assumptions about the inferiority of women that undermine healthy relationships.

At the heart of dominance theory is the asymmetrical structure of society in which that which is associated with males is valued more highly than that which is associated with females. The theory claims that if we are to have egalitarian relationships among women and men, we must change the economic and political structures that perpetuate male domination of women.

Two-Cultures Theory

In contrast to dominance theory, the second theory emphasizes the different ways boys and girls are socialized in same-sex play groups during the years when children are developing their communication competence.[14] Different communication strategies are rewarded in female groups than in male groups. Advocates of this theory believe that differences in perspective and experience are so great that boys and girls can best be thought of as members of different cultures. One of the best-sellers based on the two-cultures theory captures the point in its title *Men Are from Mars, Women Are from Venus*.[15]

From this perspective, problems in male-female interaction stem from miscommunication that inevitably occurs when people of different cultures interact. In female culture, girls learn cooperative communication strategies that contribute to harmony in relationships. They learn to offer indirect rather than direct criticism and develop empathic skills that help them interpret one another accurately and sensitively. This early socialization leads women to value communication that creates and sustains relationships.

In contrast to the values of harmony and connection emphasized in female culture, male peer groups emphasize competition. Boys are rewarded for telling stories and jokes in skillful ways so they can hold an audience. Boys are ranked more highly if they are able to dominate other boys by talking more and interrupting them. A boy gains status if he states his opinions confidently, without qualifiers, and if others do not challenge him.[16]

According to the two-cultures theory, the communication strategies we learned as children dominate our communication repertoire as adults. Men and women tend to use the communication style that served them well as children. Each communication style is valid and reasonable in its own right. It is just that the goals and strategies of the two styles conflict. The key, according to linguist Deborah Tannen, is for women and men to understand what is happening and not assign malicious intent to one another.[17] Men and women are encouraged to develop flexibility and increase their repertoire of communication strategies.

Tannen is a well-respected linguist whose research has been acclaimed within her field. However, her best-sellers, which offer insights from linguistics for the general public, trouble some scholars. Psychologist Mary Crawford believes that the two-cultures theory is dangerous for women. She believes that it emphasizes miscommunication between two always well-meaning people who have simply been socialized to use different communication styles, both of which are valid. She believes Tannen fails to address the significant power differences between women and men. Her most compelling concerns focus on date-rape. If a man and woman have merely misunderstood one another, then no one is at fault. The issues of power and coercion are lost in efforts to understand how a man might have heard the woman say "no," but was sure she meant "yes." Given the violence against women that permeates our homes and communities, it is important to consider the extreme example of rape to see what can happen if the two-cultures theory is misapplied.[18]

Although dominance theory and two-cultures theory are often presented as competing explanations of differences in male-female communication, there are important insights in each theory that can advance our efforts to work together as women and men. Rather than choose between the theories, we will gain a richer and more adequate understanding if we look at the ways in which they add to and qualify one another.

Dominance theory is important because it points to ways institutionalized power differences between women and men play out in our communication with one another. It also reminds us that the consequences of misunderstandings are often more harsh for those with less power.

Although historical forces of male dominance are important, it is not sufficient to reduce all conflicts between women and men to issues of power. What the two-cultures theory offers is additional insight into differences in conversational styles that may create conflict in cases in which men are not trying to dominate or control the situation. Although two-cultures theory can be developed without including an analysis of power, it does not preclude such analysis. Intercultural communication scholars remind us that communication between people of different cultures must include an analysis of power also. When people from one culture have historically dominated another group, communication between individuals is affected by that history.

A final caution must be applied to the use of any research. Research helps us understand patterns in male and female communication, but there is significant variation among women, just as there is among men. As Christians seeking to renew the church, we need to focus on seeing each person as an individual rather than relating to anyone only as a member of a group defined by gender, age, race, or ethnicity.

Recommendations for Small Groups in the Church

1. Talk with others about the kind of Christian community you believe we are called to create. What are the implications of your vision for communication in groups?
2. List the small groups associated with your church.
   a. Who is in each group? Who leads it? What happens in the meetings?
   b. Which groups are led by women? Have leaders been trained?
   c. Meet with group members to talk about the importance of communication in every group.
3. Think of mixed-sex small groups you have been part of in the church. Identify the most effective and least effective ones. Why was the one experience so much different than the other?
4. Ask a group in which you currently participate to reflect intentionally on their communication.
   a. What do you think is particularly effective about their communication? What could be improved? Start with what group members are doing well. The problems are so obvious to us we often fail to identify the good things that are happening. Write comments on a flip chart for future discussion.
   b. Do women and men in the group communicate differently?
   c. Because nonverbal behavior is so critical, and we often are unaware of our own nonverbal behavior, videotape a regular meeting and view it together. Turn the sound off so people focus on nonverbal behavior. It is useful to have close-ups of individuals speaking, but also include frequent shots of the whole group, so you can note the nonverbal responses people make to one another.
   d. Read books on small group communication and gender differences in communication and discuss them together.[19]

    e. Encourage groups to reflect periodically on how the group is doing. What do group members like about the group? What do they wish were different?

5. If a group deals with matters that can cause conflict, encourage the group to agree to a process to use if conflict begins to be destructive. For example, if a group meets to discuss an emotional issue such as the ordination of gay and lesbian members, agree on rules for communication that will help the group to focus on issues and not attack one another. Try to agree ahead of time on a process to use if conflict begins to be destructive. For example, one person may be assigned the role of calling for a break in the discussion in order for the group to take ten minutes for silent prayer before continuing. We can use such prayer to ask God's help that we not destroy one another. Conflicts need to be faced, but the way we do it is critical. Angry words spoken without thinking can damage relationships beyond repair.

6. In any group in which you participate, be responsible for contributing to the group constructively. Listen carefully to others. Monitor the amount of your participation. Ask people who are being left out of the process what they think, and encourage their participation.

7. Regardless of the task that brings the group together, use the spiritual basis for the group explicitly. Pray together, including prayers for the group itself. Encourage group members to pray for one another when they are apart. The human role in church renewal is critical, but may we never forget to invoke the healing, creative power of the Holy Spirit to guide and support our efforts.

Notes

1. Susan B. Shimanoff and Mercilee M. Jenkins, "Leadership and Gender: Challenging Assumptions and Recognizing Resources," in *Small Group Communication: Theory and Practice,* ed. Robert S. Cathcart, Larry A. Samovar, and Linda D. Henman (Madison: Brown and Benchmark, 1996), 327–44.
2. The social-constructionist perspective points to ways in which reality is socially constructed. In extreme form, it leads to the view that all truth is relative. However, one can appreciate the ways in which reality is socially constructed while rejecting the conclusion that there is no correspondence between truth and any actual reality. Paying attention to the ways in which the church is socially constructed does not preclude belief in God as an actual agent in creating and sustaining the church. For exam-

ples of the social-constructionist perspective in philosophy and sociology respectively, see John R. Searle, *The Construction of Social Reality* (New York: Free Press, 1995); Peter Berger and Thomas Luckmann, *The Social Construction of Reality* (New York: Anchor Press, 1966).

3. Nancy Frazier and Myra Sadker, *Sexism in School and Society* (New York: Harper & Row, 1973).

4. Carl Weick, *The Social Psychology of Organizing,* 2d ed. (Reading, Pa.: Addison-Wesley, 1979); cf. the special section discussing Weick's work in *Communication Studies* 40 (Winter 1989): 231–65.

5. Robert Wuthnow, *Sharing the Journey: Support Groups and America's New Quest for Community* (New York: Free Press, 1994), 342.

6. Paul Watzlawick, Janet Beavin, and Don Jackson, *Pragmatics of Human Communication* (New York: W. W. Norton, 1967). Although communication scholars have nuanced some of the claims made in this text, it remains one of the most influential perspectives in the study of human communication.

7. Frank E. Millar and L. Edna Rogers, "Relational Dimensions of Interpersonal Dynamics," in *Interpersonal Processes: New Directions in Communication Research,* ed. Michael E. Roloff and Gerald R. Miller (Newbury Park, Calif.: Sage Publishing, 1987), 117–39.

8. Deborah James and Janice Drakich, "Understanding Gender Differences in Amount of Talk: A Critical Review of Research," in *Gender and Conversational Interaction,* ed. Deborah Tannen (New York: Oxford University Press, 1993), 281–312.

9. Deborah Tannen, *You Just Don't Understand: Women and Men in Conversation* (New York: Ballantine Books, 1990), 78.

10. Dale Spender, *The Writing of the Sex* (New York: Pergamon, 1989), 9.

11. Kathleen Hall Jamieson, *Beyond the Double Bind: Women and Leadership* (New York: Oxford University Press, 1995), 80–81.

12. Ibid., 84.

13. See, for example, Mary Crawford, *Talking Difference: On Gender and Language* (London: Sage, 1995).

14. Daniel N. Maltz and Ruth A. Borker, "A Cultural Approach to Male-Female Miscommunication," in *Language and Social Identity,* ed. John Gumperz (Cambridge: Cambridge University Press, 1982), 192–216.

15. John Gray, *Men Are from Mars, Women Are from Venus* (New York: HarperCollins, 1992).

16. Crawford, *Talking Difference,* 88.

17. Tannen, *You Just Don't Understand,* 47.

18. Crawford, *Talking Distance,* 123–28.

19. A good book that covers basic principles of small group communication is Ernest G. Bormann and Nancy C. Bormann, *Effective Small Group Communication,* 4th ed. (Edina, Minn.: Burgess, 1988). For gender and communication, consider Deborah Tannen, *Talking from Nine to Five: Women and Men in the Workplace: Language, Sex and Power* (New York: Avon, 1994).

12

Power and Desire: Sexual Misconduct Involving Pastors and Parishioners

The moral issues addressed by pastoral theologians have shifted in the 1990s. Whereas the 1980s were concerned with narcissism and "expressive individualism," today the issues center around human sexuality. The focus of reflection is on sexual identity (especially non-heterosexual forms) and sexual misconduct (mainly heterosexual) between pastors (usually men) and parishioners (usually women). In general, pastoral theologians have taken a positive view of gay and lesbian "lifestyles," advocating tolerance and support for gays and lesbians in the name of Christian love and communal inclusiveness. Their response to the sexual misconduct issue has been considerably more mixed. In general, they have taken the view that sexual misconduct by male pastors is fundamentally an abuse of power, and they have therefore viewed the parishioners (usually women) as the primary victims and the congregation as the secondary victim of this betrayal of trust.[1]

Because the issue of power had not been a significant feature of the psychological theories traditionally employed by pastoral theologians, the critique of psychology that began in the 1980s with the narcissism issue has been carried over in the 1990s with the sexual misconduct issue. I am arguing here that we should not be so quick to dismiss psychology from our discussions of the sexual misconduct issue. It has important things to say about the issue, even as it had important things to contribute to the narcissism discussion of the 1980s.[2] Specifically, it adds a vital dimension to the current discussion of sexual misconduct by inviting us to view the issue as, to be sure, a matter of power, but also as a matter of sexual desire.

At first glance, introducing the matter of desire into the discussion may appear to obfuscate the moral issues involved and weaken the ethical arguments currently in place, but I hope to show that the ethical argument is actually strengthened by taking the role of sexual desire seriously. In this way, our prospects for finding ways to reduce the problem of sexual misconduct in congregations will be greatly enhanced. The power analyses currently in place emphasize the fear of exposure and punishment by higher judicatories as the best deterrent to pastor-initiated sexual misconduct.[3] By

Donald Capps

taking sexual desire more seriously, additional remedies present themselves.

To set the context for my argument, I will first discuss the power analyses of sexual misconduct presented by two pastoral theologians, James Newton Poling and Larry Kent Graham.

Sexual Misconduct as Abuse
of Professional Power

In his book *The Abuse of Power,* Poling distinguishes between two types of power: *relational* and *unilateral*. Relational power, or "power in its ideal form," is based on the recognition that "power is actually organized by the relational webs of which we are a part. Our ability to act in effective ways depends on our connections with other persons, and with the institutions and ideas that form the basis of our experience. Power is gauged by the complexity of the relationships that can be contained in an interaction. . . . When power is seen as the energy of the relational web itself, then power can be understood as the ability to sustain internal relationships and increase the power of the relational web as a whole."[4] Poling concludes that the "ideal direction of power in human life that is undistorted by sin and evil is toward communion and enlarged freedom; in the relational process, human bonding grows stronger and individuals and groups increase their freedom."[5]

Unilateral power is the opposite of relational power. It is the ability to produce an effect on another with only minimal impact on oneself. It emphasizes the strength of one's capacity to influence others. Poling views patriarchy as a structure for domination that creates the conditions for abuse of power. While his book focuses primarily on abuses of power by parents and husbands, he devotes a brief, concluding chapter to the implications of the abuse of power for ministry practice and offers several principles to guide both church and society in addressing such abuses. He emphasizes the need for methods for handling disclosures of sexual violence "so that men are confronted with their abuses" and for "clear ethical norms for sexual misconduct that emphasize its destructive nature and do not confuse violence with sexual activity."[6] I will return later to this way of articulating the ethical issue.

In a subsequent book coauthored with Marie M. Fortune, Poling gives more direct attention to the professional context in which sexual misconduct occurs. In the first of Poling's two chapters, he gives an account of his personal disillusionment with his mentors who abused women in their pastoral counseling relationships. He focuses on the role of theological concepts in emboldening some (mainly men) to abuse their power and others (mostly women) to suffer abuse in silence. He argues that when male pastors sexualize their relationships, they replicate "the dynamics of the drama between a patriarchal God and an obedient, self-sacrificing Jesus standing in for a sinful humanity." In religious terms, "the clergyman has taken the place of God who is all-knowing, all-powerful, and all-loving, and the parishioner has taken the place of Jesus who takes on the sins of humanity, submits her will to God's, sacrifices her life unto death on the cross for the sake of the relationship."[7]

In his second chapter, Poling focuses on his own accountability as a white male who has been part of the silent conspiracy about the sexual violence of men. Given this earlier failure, men in his judgment must meet certain conditions if they are now to speak out, one being a reliance on feminist and womanist methods of sociopolitical analysis, which are seen as preferable to psychological methods of analysis. The latter fail to include "power analysis of gender relationships and social institutions of sexuality," and, therefore, "issues of abuse disappear into the background."[8] The psychological methods of analysis that Poling has in mind are theories of intimacy and sexuality which, in his view, obscure that what is really going on is power and its abuses.

In his book *Care of Persons, Care of Worlds,* Larry Kent Graham provides an in-depth analysis of a small, activist Mennonite congregation that he served as a consultant after the pastor's resignation over allegations of sexual misconduct. The controversy had begun when a female member confided to a study group that a year earlier the pastor had made sexual advances to her when they were alone in a house on a work trip. Her disclosure brought to light that the pastor had initiated "intimate sexual caressing" with several women in the context of pastoral counseling. In private conversations with members of the congregation, he acknowledged similar behavior with twelve women over the years. Although he made general apologies and requests for forgiveness, those who spoke with him in private felt he was neither genuinely remorseful nor repentant, for he justified his actions on the grounds that what took place was "a higher form of spiritual love and those who do not understand it are not as spiritually advanced."[9]

In his "psychosystemic analysis" of this case, Graham asserts that "the core issue is a power struggle between contextual creativity and contextual organization." By contextual creativity, he means "the pervasive capacity for change which is built into reality, however limited it may be in particular cases"; and by contextual organization, he means "the identifiable continuity of the system as a whole, and of each subsystem or entity comprising the system."[10] It reflects the organizational pressures toward homeostasis, or the tendency of the system to continue to replicate itself. Graham identifies several dynamics within this contextual power struggle, including the fact that "strong-willed and strong-minded individuals dominated what was supposed to be a communal process," with the congregation polarizing into three groups: those who were "projectively bonded" with the victims and social justice; those who were "projectively bonded" with the minister and wanted him to be accountable on the one hand and not victimized on the other; and those who were "projectively bonded" with the congregation itself and did not want this situation to divide it or diminish its ministry. The struggle and tensions between these three groups were exacerbated by the minister's claim that he was the victim of the anger of women who began to speak out against him: "Some members of the church identified his pain as the pain of abuse, while others identified it as the pain of accountability. The need to clarify power accountabilities was paramount at this time. Because of intractable power arrangements, fueled by sexism, it was impossible to do so."[11]

Graham notes that when the matter was just coming to light, the congregation experienced great difficulty in knowing how to name the problem: "Early on, there was a wide range of opinion: some saw this as sexual indiscretion or inappropriate touching, others as abuse of power, others as sexual abuse, others as seduction on the part of the women, and so on." However, "To its credit, the congregation came to identify the events as an abuse of the role and power of the pastoral office by the pastor's inducting parishioners into a sexualized relationship in the name of the ministry."[12] In his role as consultant, Graham did not disclose his own view until the second feedback session:

> At that time, I shared my conviction that the main ethical issue here was that the minister violated the integrity of the pastoral office and abused the unequal power differential between the professional minister and vulnerable parishioners by inappropriately sexualizing the pastoral relationship without the presence of genuine mutual consent. In my view, which is heavily influenced by Marie Fortune, it was the minister's role to keep such events from occurring, and that he must accept the full responsibility for his behaviors and for setting the subsequent dynamics into motion.[13]

Here, Graham introduces the principle of the inequality of power that has played the central role in ethical discussions of the sexual misconduct issue.

The Paradox of Pastoral Power

Karen Lebacqz and Ronald G. Barton's *Sex in the Parish* argues that in the congregational context the crucial issue is the parishioner's *freedom* to consent to sexual intimacy with the pastor.[14] Such freedom should be assumed to be limited or nonexistent where there is an *inequality of power between the two parties*. Because pastors have the power as professionals and parishioners as parishioners do not, we must assume that in the vast majority of cases parishioners are not in a position to consent freely in sit-

uations involving sexual behavior with their pastors. They emphasize that
the issue is not the *perceived* power of the pastor, but the *actual* power.
Perceived power is deceptive, because pastors often do not perceive themselves to have power. When they look at their secular counterparts, who
command higher salaries and enjoy higher social prestige, they do not *feel*
powerful but relatively power*less*. Nor is the issue whether the parishioner
has greater power *outside this relationship* (e.g., is financially better off,
comes from a "better" or "more prestigious" family background, and so
forth). These are irrelevant to the power differential in the pastor-parishioner
relationship. In this relationship the pastor as the professional has the
greater power, because the power differential favors the professional. In
a relationship in which one is the professional and the other is not, the
sole issue is whether the nonprofessional is in a position to consent freely,
and where a power differential exists, there can be no free consent. Even
in instances where the parishioner might initiate the sexual advance, this
does not affect the power differential. Abuse of power is not thereby eliminated or even compromised.

Lebacqz and Barton consider the ministerial profession especially vul-
nerable to sexual misconduct because of the nature of its unique powers.[15]
Pastors have the *power of freedom,* that is, the power that comes with not
being under the continual supervision or surveillance of others; and they
have the *power of access and accessibility,* that is, the privileged access to
the personal lives of parishioners that comes with being in a profession
long associated with giving care. I would add to these two powers a third
one that is implied in the second, the *power of knowledge.* Pastors come
to know a great deal about the families in their congregations and often
know the sorts of things that it takes a therapist several weeks to learn
about their clients. Pastors may not consciously exploit this knowledge,
but sometimes they do so unconsciously. If, for example, a pastor is aware
that the husband of a parishioner is inferior to her in intellectual and social skills, he may unwittingly "one-up" her husband by meeting her needs
for someone intelligent and understanding with whom to talk.

Because these are the unique powers of the professional minister, this
raises the issue of what I call "the paradox of pastoral power." While there
are many pastors who are on power trips and who demonstrate their
power through premeditated sexual exploitation, there are other pastors
who become involved in an affair as a direct consequence of their efforts
to reduce the power differential between the pastor and the parishioner.
As Marilyn Peterson points out, affairs between pastors and parishioners
often begin with the pastor expressing concern for the situation of the
parishioner (e.g., a troubled marriage, a demoralizing family problem),
which is then followed by the pastor being queried or volunteering similar information about his marriage and family situation, and, with this, a
bond between them is formed, leading, in some cases, to a sexual liaison.[16]

Thus, pastors who make a conscious effort to reduce the power differential between themselves and a parishioner—by taking personal interest in the other and by engaging in mutual self-disclosure—are at greater risk of becoming sexually involved with a parishioner.

These are pastors who do not insist on standing on a pastoral pedestal but who, on the contrary, make an effort to reduce the power differential: "Don't call me Reverend, just call me Bob." Yet, what needs to be recognized (and seldom is) is that such efforts to reduce the power differential actually increase it. Why? Because power in ministry is precisely the power of freedom, of access and accessibility, and of knowledge. Thus, as the parishioner shares intimate facts about herself, making her personal life accessible to him, the power differential is actually increased, appearances to the contrary notwithstanding. And if the pastor proceeds to share intimate facts about himself, this does nothing to counteract the increase in the power differential, because, through these self-disclosures, his access and accessibility to the parishioner are greater than ever. This is what I call the *paradox of pastoral power:* "The more you succeed in reducing the power differential between you and the parishioner, the greater it becomes." Then, of course, Lebacqz and Barton's ethical maxim applies: Where there is a power differential between two adults, we must assume that the one who has less power is not free to consent, appearances notwithstanding.

We in the pastoral theology field must bear some of the responsibility for failing to couple our encouragement of a more "personal" and "attentive" pastoral style with cautions and warnings that this more personal style will increase, not decrease, the power differential between pastor and parishioner. Moreover, those who have advocated the "empowerment of the laity," and who have attempted to minimize or erase the distinction between pastoral and lay ministry—those who have challenged the "clerical paradigm"—must also bear some responsibility as well. Their initiatives have contributed to the illusion that the power differential between pastor and parishioner may be set aside if not eliminated altogether.

The Role of Desire in Cases
of Sexual Misconduct

The ethical principle that where a power differential is present, the one whose power is limited or nonexistent does not have the freedom to consent, provides a sound basis on which to begin the process of establishing responsibility and accountability in cases of sexual misconduct involving pastors and parishioners. In the case discussed by Graham, it led to clarification of the issue—how to name what has been going on—that had been the focus of so much dispute, anger, and recrimination among the members. On the other hand, this articulation of a clearly stated ethical norm tends to silence those individuals in the congregation who saw the matter as adultery and/or affairs between consenting adults, as sexual indiscretion or inappropriate touching, or even as seduction on the part of the women. If one is concerned about the fact that strong-willed and strong-minded individuals dominated what was supposed to be a communal process, ought one not also be concerned about the power of a clearly articulated ethical principle to settle the issue, once and for all?

Reaching clarity about the ethical issue of the abuse of power did allow the congregation to reach closure on the matter and get on with its life. Nevertheless, still further analysis of the many factors at work in this case suggests that more than abusing power was at stake. Acknowledging these factors—especially desire—may alert us to new ways to avoid pastoral misconduct.

The primary theoretical resource for my way of approaching this matter is the French philosopher, Michel Foucault, who emphasizes the complexities of power relations. He views power as "'the multiplicity of power relations' at work in a particular area." Alan Sheridan explains: "These power relations are the object of an unceasing struggle in which they are transformed, strengthened, and, sometimes, reversed. It is not something that can be acquired, seized, or shared. It is exercised from innumerable points, in a set of unequal, shifting relations. Power comes as much from below as from above. Power relations do not exist outside other types of relation (those found in economic processes, in the diffusion of knowledge, in sexual relations), but are imminent in them." Foucault also claimed that power relations are not governed by an "opposition between dominators and dominated, which is then reproduced from top to bottom in ever smaller groupings, but are formed and operate in places of work, families, institutions, groups of all kinds, etc., and serve as the supports for the broad effects of division that run through the whole of society."[17] Thus, power relations are not attributable to a single individual or even to a ruling group, "but arise in an apparently anonymous way from the local situations in which they first appear." Resistance always accompanies power, not, however, in the sense of an external, contrary force, but by the very fact that power exists: "Power relations depend on a multiplicity of points of resistance, which serve at once as adversary, target, support, foothold. Just as there is no center of power, there is no center of revolt. . . . There is a plurality of resistances, each a special case, distributed in an irregular way in time and space."[18]

This view of power does not challenge the view that there are "power differentials" in any given situation, but it cautions against viewing these differentials as fixed rather than as fluid and transitory. Thus, although it is true that there is a power differential in the pastoral counseling setting, and that this differential favors the professional, it may also be true that, in other contexts, the power differential is weighted in favor of parishioners.

Foucault also notes that sexuality and power have been related, in complex ways, throughout human history: "Pleasure and power do not cancel each other out; nor do they turn against one another; they pursue, overlap and reinforce one another. They are linked together by complex, positive mechanisms of excitation and incitement."[19] In short, desire and power are inseparable, and this means that we need to exercise a healthy suspicion when anyone, in the interests of ethical clarity, claims that sexual desire is not an issue, that the issue is simply and purely a matter of power. Furthermore, because Foucault's view of how power relations actually work is quite similar to the "relational" model of power advocated by Poling and Graham, the question is whether it makes any sense to view this model as the ideal, as that for which we are striving, when this is already for the most part what we have.

In practical terms, this means that solutions to problems of sexual misconduct may not lie in efforts to achieve a more relational (that is, equally balanced) distribution of power, but they may instead lie in taking the issue of sexual desire seriously, both by analyzing it as carefully as we analyze power relations and by using such analyses to inform our search for better solutions to these problems.

In *The Age of Desire*, psychoanalyst Joel Koval discusses how, in its original form (that is, the experience of infants), desire "consists of striving toward an object that cannot yet be named."[20] The infant experiences a sense of lack but does not yet know what it is that she longs for, pines after. In time, she identifies the "other"—usually mother—as the "object" of her desire. Thus, at first, desire is an undifferentiated emotion that then becomes focused on a particular object selected or chosen from the vast array of objects that make up one's world. No doubt, this focusing of desire goes hand in hand with the development, in the infant, of increasing visual acuity, the ability of the eyes to identify discrete objects in the external world.

Koval further suggests that desire involves the naming of objects from the standpoint of self-appropriation. Mother is "*my* mother." Thus, "Without desire, the world consists only of things, inert masses. Desire makes of inert things 'things-for-us,' that is, objects. Desire is therefore a constitution of both self and object."[21] This means that desire is more than a subjective or intrapsychic process, for if the desire is to come to fruition, the external world must be altered. If the object of the infant's desire is "*my* mother," then she must acknowledge the infant as "*my* child." In fact, it was her desire that originally constituted the infant as "*my* child." The process thus involves mutual self-appropriations of objects in cases where two living beings desire one another.

Koval discusses the situation in which desire is not reciprocated and suggests that typically in such instances desire takes the form of hate as one attempts to destroy the other to avenge this injury to self.[22] In this, and various other ways, desire can become pathological, symptomatic of unmet expectations from the external world of objects. A more mature way of responding to desire's frustration, however, is to recognize that the world comprises other objects that are capable of inspiring self-appropriations. Much of what occurs in psychoanalysis is the reeducation of desire, training in the art of recognizing the value and worth of objects one did not originally long for. In essence, this is the psychoanalytic theory of sublimation, and it is offered in place of either the hopeless enterprise of destroying the original object (desire transformed into hatred) or the repression of desire altogether.

In his discussion of desire, James R. Kincaid claims that the Victorians, whom we usually accuse of being sexually repressed, were actually more enlightened than we are about desire. They understood that desire often affords greater pleasure when it remains in the state of longing—free-floating—and does not attempt to fulfill itself by realizing an instrumental objective. The Victorians were capable of admiring from afar. The pleasure here derives largely from the fact that if desire remains in limbo, so to speak, it remains free from the power relations that often lead to the distortion and misdirection of desire.[23]

Even in this thumbnail sketch of desire, its relevance to cases of sexual misconduct similar to the one discussed by Graham should be apparent. The minister in Graham's case would have saved himself and others (including his own family) great grief had he undergone training in the reeducation of his sexual desire. One of the redirections that Freud himself advocated was an appreciation for art and its objects of value and beauty. In the context of art, one may "own" one's sexual desires in a way that does not result in the transformation of unreciprocated desire into hatred. Developing an interest in the visual arts, poetry, music, and architecture provides some of the ways in which pastors may redirect their sexual desires.

The minister might also have developed a tolerance for the *non*fulfillment of sexual desire, for holding desire in limbo. Of course, "limbo" was originally a religious term. In contrast to purgatory, it was the place "for human beings not weighed down by any personal sin but only by original sin" (e.g., children who died without benefit of baptism or righteous souls who predated Christ). For these, limbo was conceived as the bosom of Abraham, a place, like a mother's womb, of calm and tranquil peace.[24] Limbo is much preferable to purgatory.

Moreover, the implied threat of the transformation of desire into hatred was the basis for the minister's ability to enforce a woman's silence. If pastoral powers of freedom, access and accessibility, and knowledge provide the necessary conditions for sexual abuse, the threat of the transformation of desire into hatred enables the sexual abuse to persist. In effect, the pastor now enjoys the power to destroy.

Another point, more controversial, is that the minister's desire *might* (I emphasize *might*) have been reciprocated by one or more of the women. If so, this does not affect in any way the ethical argument that, where there is a power differential involved, there is no freedom of consent, and, therefore, the pastor's behavior was wrong. Still, it is important that women, no less than men, be allowed to "own" their sexual desires. They should not be required to disown them as the price to be paid for speaking out against, and making disclosures of, pastoral abuses of power.

Finally, note the deficiencies in the discourse of desire that prevailed in the Mennonite congregation cited by Graham. These deficiencies were evident in the minister's claim that he was offering the women a higher "spiritual love," implying that sexual desire in its natural form is not good enough. They were also evident in one of the women's statements that her experience of being counseled by the pastor "clearly included gratification of sexual appetite which I knew then and now was appropriate only to your wife and required an agreement to secrecy."[25] The language of "gratification" may be accurate in this instance, for it captures the power aspect involved; but it conveys that sexual desire, even in the husband-wife relationship, is appetitive, and says nothing about desire as a mutual self-appropriation between two living—and loving—beings. In my view, the Christian community itself bears some of the responsibility for cases of sexual misconduct because it has failed to develop a discourse of desire that is truly worthy of itself.

Problem-Solving versus
Relationship-Oriented Counseling

For a pastoral theologian, it is profoundly disturbing that sexual misconduct typically originates in the pastoral counseling setting. This should prompt pastoral theologians to be ever vigilant about what they write and teach about the nature of pastoral counseling. For example, William B. Oglesby, Jr., emphasizes the "relational encounter" between the pastor and parishioner on the grounds that "the person is always more important than the problem, and the relationship is more important than the solution." Because parishioners often resist genuine relationship with others, the pastor's role is to challenge them to enter into relationship: "The minister is aware that if the encounter does not happen in the relationship with the parishioner, it is not likely to happen at all. It probably will not occur 'out there' unless it is experienced 'in here.'"[26]

While well-intended, this relationship model of pastoral counseling is itself subject to abuse and even to honest confusion about what the pastor is expected to do—and to be—in the pastoral counseling context. With no apologies, therefore, I have advocated from the very beginning of my own career as a pastoral theologian the "problem-solving" approach. This model emphasizes that pastoral counseling should be brief (one to three sessions) and that the pastoral relationship itself (that is, what goes on "in here") is not the locus of change. Change occurs as the parishioner begins to experience herself ("out there") as a capable problem-solver. The fact that it took so long for the women in the Graham case to redress their grievances is proof that the minister did not help them to become their own problem-solvers. The pastor's task in pastoral counseling is to help the parishioner focus on that aspect of the problem for which there is a clearly identifiable solution, and to use this initial success as basis for tackling the problem's more difficult features. If problem-solving counseling does not focus on the pastoral relationship itself, boundary violations are much less likely to occur.

Notes

1. See esp. Marie M. Fortune, *Is Nothing Sacred? When Sex Invades the Pastoral Relationship* (New York: HarperCollins, 1989).
2. See Donald Capps, *The Depleted Self: Sin in a Narcissistic Age* (Minneapolis: Fortress Press, 1993).
3. See Marie M. Fortune and James N. Poling, *Sexual Abuse by Clergy: A Crisis for the Church* (Decatur, Ga.: Journal of Pastoral Care Publications, 1994).
4. James Newton Poling, *The Abuse of Power: A Theological Problem* (Nashville: Abingdon Press, 1991), 24–25.
5. Ibid., 27.
6. Ibid., 184–85.
7. Fortune and Poling, *Sexual Abuse by Clergy,* 39.
8. Ibid., 51.
9. Larry Kent Graham, *Care of Persons, Care of Worlds: A Psychosystem Approach to Pastoral Care and Counseling* (Nashville: Abingdon Press, 1992), 228.
10. Ibid., 231, 259–60.
11. Ibid., 233.
12. Ibid.
13. Ibid., 257–58.
14. Karen Lebacqz and Ronald G. Barton, *Sex in the Parish* (Louisville: Westminster/John Knox Press, 1991).
15. Lebacqz and Barton's survey of pastors indicates that the incidence of sexual misconduct among pastors is 13 percent, whereas among psychotherapists it is 5 percent.
16. Marilyn Peterson, cited in *The Lutheran* (June 1993): 28. See also her book *At Personal Risk: Boundary Violations in Professional-Client Relationships* (New York: W. W. Norton, 1992).
17. Alan Sheridan, *Michel Foucault: The Will to Truth* (London and New York: Routledge, 1990), 184.

18. Ibid., 184–85.
19. Foucault, quoted in Sheridan, 176.
20. Joel Koval, *The Age of Desire: Reflections of a Radical Psychoanalyst* (New York: Pantheon Books, 1981), 70.
21. Ibid., 81.
22. Ibid., 104.
23. James R. Kincaid, *Child-Loving: The Erotic Child and Victorian Culture* (New York and London: Routledge, 1992), 31.
24. Jacques Le Goff, *The Birth of Purgatory,* trans. Arthur Goldhammer (Chicago: University of Chicago Press, 1984), 158, 220–21.
25. Graham, *Care of Persons, Care of Worlds,* 227.
26. William B. Oglesby, Jr., *Biblical Themes for Pastoral Care* (Nashville: Abingdon Press, 1980), 41, 87–88.

13

Reclaiming Ourselves:
A Spirituality for Women's Empowerment

The greatest hazard of all, losing the self, can occur very quietly in the world, as if it were nothing at all. No other loss can occur so quietly; any other loss—an arm, a leg, five dollars, a [spouse], etc.—is sure to be noticed.

—Søren Kierkegaard, *The Sickness Unto Death*

Girls and the Loss Of Self: Someone Noticed

The mother of one of my daughter's friends approached me one day very troubled. "What exactly do you Presbyterians believe, anyway?" she asked. She then told me about a conversation she had overheard between her daughter and several other twelve-year-old girls. The girls were sitting in a fast-food restaurant; the mother was seated at the next table, ostensibly reading the newspaper. One after another the girls expressed disapproval of themselves. They were not nice enough, not good enough, not pretty enough, not smart enough, and not thin enough. This mother listened with growing horror. Finally, she could take it no longer and crashed the conversation. "I can't believe you girls are saying these things. You should be proud of yourselves; you should feel good about who you are; you should confidently announce yourselves to the world!" she exclaimed. One girl, Joanne, in utter seriousness, responded, "I can't be proud of myself, it's against my religion. Pride is a sin." "What religion is that?" the mother queried. "I'm Presbyterian," the girl stated matter-of-factly and then repeated her point, "we don't believe in pride."

Joanne, I knew, was a very active churchgoer, reared in a mainline, middle-of-the-road, sometimes liberal-leaning congregation. This church had fought to give this girl the possibility of becoming an ordained elder or minister of Word and sacrament, as well as having equal rights in society.

And yet, without realizing it, the church was also enculturating her toward self-loss by repeatedly emphasizing the sin of pride and self-assertion. Over years of hearing sermons, attending Sunday school, and taking part in numerous practices of the church, Joanne had (mis)learned that feeling good about herself and asserting her confidence was something that got in the way of her relationship with God; it was sin.

In North American culture, gender training encourages self-loss in girls. In this chapter, I want to empower girls and women to reclaim themselves by confronting those theological teachings and practices that overemphasize the sin of pride and overpromote the virtues of humility and self-abasement for girls and women. Although we commonly find this tendency in Protestant theology, it is by no means unique to Protestantism; many Christian traditions are culpable here. Certainly, there is an important place for humility in Christian spirituality, but if we promote humility to the exclusion of confidence, then we particularly put Christian girls in peril.[1]

Girls and Gendering Rites:
Giving Our Daughters Away

A couple of years ago, the *Wall Street Journal* ran a short article on awards given at a graduation ceremony for kindergartners.[2] A New Jersey father, the article related, was chagrined to discover that his young daughter's school, nestled in a progressive suburb of New York City, had created strikingly gender-stereotyped awards. The boys' awards were: Very Best Thinker, Most Eager Learner, Most Imaginative, Most Enthusiastic, Most Scientific, Best Friend, Mr. Personality, Hardest Worker, and Best Sense of Humor. The girls' awards were: All-Around Sweetheart, Sweetest Personality, Cutest Personality, Best Sharer, Best Artist, Biggest Heart, Best Manners, Best Helper, and Most Creative. The boys were affirmed for their intellectual abilities; the girls for their sweetness! These were five-year-olds completing perhaps their most significant experience in public socialization. When I think of Robert Fulghum's claim that "all I really need to know I learned in kindergarten," I shudder.[3] If these are the awards with which the year culminates, these girls were reinforced toward these specified ends all year long. While the boys were shaped into hardworking, enthusiastic, and imaginative learners, the girls were molded into sweet, well-mannered, cute, and helpful young ladies. If this was only noticed in 1994, then how many previous years included this gendering rite?[4] If all that girls are supposed to know about being a woman is learned in kindergarten, their lessons can lead to later disempowerment. Moreover, research on adolescent girls suggests that these gender rites continue even into the teenage years. Numerous studies document the way in which girls are prone to silence their own feelings and viewpoints in order to accommodate themselves to the needs and feelings of others.[5]

Afflicting Miriam and
Her Daughters: The Church and Women

For some girls like Joanne, these disempowering lessons are reinforced in church. As a junior-high Sunday school teacher who is also the mother of a junior-high girl, I bring concerns for girls' development to my leadership. Recently, while perusing curriculum for my Sunday school class, I came across a lesson that could clinch Joanne's humility training. The lesson titled "Leprosy!" is from Numbers 12.[6] In this narrative of Israel's journey toward the Promised Land, we read of a leadership struggle involving Moses, Aaron, and Miriam. Critical of their brother Moses for marrying a foreign woman, Miriam and Aaron ask, "Has the Lord spoken only through Moses? Has he not spoken through us also?" The Lord is angered that these two challenge Moses' authority. Inexplicably, the Lord punishes Miriam alone, giving her the most dreaded of diseases, leprosy, which forces her outside of the community. Through the intercession of Moses and Aaron, the sentence is limited to seven days. The community waits for Miriam to heal before they march on.

The lesson on this passage begins in a very promising manner, with an exercise in recovering earlier stories about Miriam, which affirm her role in the life of the people. However, it then moves in a regrettable direction. In the students' booklet, the youth are instructed to understand that Miriam, granted important gifts of her own, is punished because she overstepped her bounds. She traveled "three small steps to ruin: envy, anger, rebellion." And thus, if we look through the eyes of the biblical writer, the youth are informed, "we need to understand that Miriam's punishment was extremely appropriate for her transgression." By seeking to exalt herself, Miriam threatened to divide the community, and she was therefore rightly shut out of the community for a time. Acknowledging evidence of sexism and then immediately dismissing its relevance for the story, the writers stress that servant leadership is at issue—Miriam refused to be a humble servant. Miriam's gifts were "empathy and the ability to express herself verbally and musically through dance, instruments, and singing"; but Moses alone was the leader and the decision maker. "There seems to be something about us that dislikes the success of others," the curriculum notes, both summarizing and personalizing the story.

The students' booklet then provides this contemporized analogy: Suppose Miriam volunteers to do a liturgical dance in place of a sermon on youth Sunday, but, instead, the group asks her brother Moses to preach. Moses gallantly offers to include the dance in the service, but Miriam is angered that she will not be the center of attention and refuses to participate. This analogy not only reinforces the interpretation that Miriam is behaving selfishly, but it underscores a point developed further by the curriculum—

that the brothers in the story are the compassionate and caring ones. The two men are held up as the heroes of the tale.

The lesson closes with a comparison between Miriam's story and our stories. "We are similar to Miriam. God has given each of us gifts. But do they create in us humility or pride? Our actions may divide or threaten to separate us from those around us." Then the learners are instructed to reflect on gifts that create in them a sense of pride and thus separate them from doing good for others. A visual illustration reinforces the point. The shaded figure of a lone female (Miriam), stooped with humiliation, is in one corner of the page; the shaded figures of gathered community members, arms folded in stern disapproval, are in the other. The image sears the message on young minds: Female assertion leads to rejection and disgrace.

Let's look more closely at the impact of this lesson on female youth.

First, consider the interpretation rendered of Miriam's actions. Certainly, the story of Miriam in Numbers 12 is complex. The biblical narrative sought to express the singular importance of Moses and the dangers of conflict and strife in the life of a threatened people. The lesson, however, makes a telling interpretive error. Although it is not clear why Miriam and Aaron challenged Moses' choice of a foreign wife, it is a gender-biased stretch (and one that goes beyond the text) to attribute it to Miriam's self-centeredness. It is a common theme throughout scripture that foreigners can threaten the unity and future of the people of God. Although this motif is theologically regrettable and not unchallenged by the scripture itself, Miriam is in good biblical company when she expresses her xenophobia. Miriam and Aaron (whose rebellion drops just as inexplicably out of the lesson as it does from God's disciplinary action) probably were concerned about upholding the unity of the community; they challenged Moses' choice of wife because they feared that a stranger would threaten the people. Although Miriam may indeed have been narrow-minded, the accusation that she was self-seeking is, I think, incorrect. Her aim was more likely the good of the people. By interpreting Miriam's actions as pride and self-seeking, we reinforce the stereotype that a woman's role is always to be compliant and empathetic and never strong and assertive, even when she has an important question to ask.

There is evidence to suggest that the community of Israel did not interpret Miriam's actions as self-seeking. In fact, the curriculum artist, by depicting the community in a menacing posture, contradicts the text of the story. There is no mention in the text that the people were angry at Miriam. Miriam is shut out of the camp for seven days, "and the people did not set out on the march until Miriam had been brought in again" (v. 15). The people waited faithfully for their ostracized sister! While it is clear in the story that God and Moses were angry with Miriam, the impression is that the people were loyal to her.

Correcting these interpretive errors does not resolve the difficulties inherent in the text. A lesson dealing with this text should wrestle with two further issues that have an impact on youth. The question posed by Aaron and Miriam is a good one: has God spoken only through one person? In the Reformed tradition, we believe that God speaks through many members of a community; we are a priesthood of believers. Our young people should be raised knowing that their questions and challenges are worthy of a hearing. Miriam raised an important question about identity boundaries, one that needs to be continually faced. Even if a community decides that inclusion rather than exclusion is the better choice, the role of questions and conflicts for deepening a community's theological reflection can be affirmed. The lesson misses this point latent in Numbers 12. As it now stands, the directed conversation between the youth and this text will discourage the full participation of youth in a community of faith. A deeper engagement would wrestle with the questions of leadership raised by the text, and it would engage this story with other Hebrew scriptures that acknowledge the wisdom and leadership potential of youth and women. It is a magnificent irony that Moses, in the preceding chapter of Numbers, chastised a young man who complained that others were prophesying in the camp: "Are you jealous for my sake? Would that all the Lord's people were prophets, and that the Lord would put his spirit on them!" (11:29).

Furthermore, the sexism in our text should be named and challenged. Male and female youth will come away believing that when boys question authority they will be frowned upon, but when girls question authority, they will be severely punished. Here, the text mirrors the way our culture often treats women, and we do well to confront the realism of the story. But we also need to recover and raise the question Miriam participates in— has not the Lord spoken through others, women, also?[7] Here is an opportunity for a group of young people to face the history of female exclusion from leadership; the story could have been an occasion for remembering others like Miriam who were silenced. The curriculum writers reinforce the silencing of girls' and women's voices by facilely assuming that female assertion is driven by envy, which leads to ruin, by affirming the severity of Miriam's punishment, and by dismissing the issue of sexism.

The lesson culminates with some questions intended to promote spiritual growth in the learners. The questions are primarily negative in their emphasis: "What gifts do I have that create in me a sense of pride and thinking that I am better than others? What have I done or said that has separated me from those I love? When have I failed to do the good that I could because I have not used my gifts on behalf of others?" By the time the fourth, constructive question is reached ("How can I use my God-given gifts creatively?"), girls will be so afraid of pride, self-assertion, and self-centeredness that the only answers they give will be self-sacrificing ones. Having identified with Miriam, whose gifts have been circumscribed as dancing and empathy, they will be disempowered from following a path that includes prophetic assertion and challenge to the status-quo leadership.

When girls get the message in their religious education that the qualities of compliance and humility are the most important Christian qualities, they become afflicted along with Miriam. When pride is the sin to be overcome and humility is the virtue to achieve, spiritual practices may, unfortunately, become "steps to ruin" for girls and women.

Spirituality and Loss of Self: Steps to Ruin

A strong emphasis on humility, obedience, and submission of the will are prevalent in many classic formulations of spiritual disciplines. An increased interest in spirituality has led to a recovery of these disciplines; those of St. Benedict, in particular, are frequently popularized. Rather than being used in the complex context for which they were created, they are often recovered and mass-marketed in reduced and simplistic ways. In a recent compilation of spiritual classics, Benedict's ladder to humility is reproduced. Here, Benedict warns that "every exaltation of ourselves is a kind of pride," and that the way of ascending the "ladder of humility" is to remove traces of pride.[8] Viewing these disciplines through the issue of women's empowerment raises serious concerns about their universal helpfulness.

According to Benedict, humility involves the recognition that "everyone who exalts himself shall be humbled; and he that humbles himself shall be exalted." The steps to humility are as follows:

1. Reverence for God: "Again, the Scriptures say, 'There are ways that seem right to us, but in the end will lead us to ruin.'"
2. Rejecting our own will and desires and, instead, doing God's will.
3. Obedience to others: "We submit ourselves to another in all obedience."
4. Enduring affliction: "Enduring with patience the injuries and afflictions we face. . . . Those who have faith must bear every disagreeable thing for the Lord."
5. Confession: "Keep no secrets from the one to whom we confess. We must humbly confess all our evil thoughts and all our evil actions."
6. Contentment: "Be content in all things . . . mindful of our own lowliness."
7. Self-reproach: "We declare with our tongue and believ[ing] in our inmost soul that we are the lowliest and vilest of all."
8. Obeying the common rule: "We do this by doing nothing except what is sanctioned by the rule and example of elders."

9. Silence: "To withhold our tongue from speaking, keeping silence until we are asked."
10. Seriousness: "We are not easily provoked to laughter."
11. Simple speech: "We are to speak gently and not with a loud voice."
12. Humble in appearance: "Our attitude should be that of the publican in the Gospel who said, with his eyes fixed on the ground, 'Lord, I am a sinner and I am not worthy to lift my eyes up to heaven.'"
13. Humility as a way of life: "We shall arrive at that love of God which, being perfect, casts out all fear."

Humility, seen as the foundation of spirituality, is understood to be the antidote to the vices of anger, ambition (seeking to control one's life), and pride. Rather than express anger at another, the spiritual person is to seek the wrong in oneself; rather than control one's life, the spiritual person is to endure patiently its suffering; rather than assert autonomy in relation to one's spiritual leaders, the spiritual person is to obey and submit. The outcome of humility is frequently named as *apatheia,* a stoic term referring to the ability to distance oneself from one's passions, egocentric compulsions, and striving needs.[9] The one with *apatheia* possesses an internal calm—even insularity—that remains undisturbed in the face of external vicissitudes.

If girls and women raised like Joanne and the New Jersey kindergartners seek spiritual direction of the type described, it can endanger their self-development. Girls, already raised to reject their own needs, are further instructed to reject their own will as inherently opposed to God's will; girls, already expected to obey men, are told to submit themselves to others in all obedience; girls, already assumed to endure subordination, are told to endure patiently everything that comes their way and to be content in all things; girls, already self-doubting, are encouraged to reproach themselves fully; girls, already hesitant to express their voices, are trained to cultivate quietness and silence as spiritual virtues. In a culture where discrimination and violence against women are prevalent, we are training women to be accomplices in the sins against them.

For those whose voices are already suppressed, Benedict's ladder can lead to a damaging intensification of suppression. When we promote an absolute understanding of obedience, we remove personal and social responsibility and produce a shallow discipleship. The motivation for Calvin's call to a knowledgeable faith that does not rest upon pious ignorance and that does not "turn over to [the church] the task of inquiring and knowing" is lost.[10] The passion for Luther's bold legacy "Here I stand!" is eviscerated, and reformation is quenched. Forced obedience to others, including religious others, results in that "greatest hazard of all, losing the self," which

147

Søren Kierkegaard exposed. It occurs so "very quietly in the world," not because it is "nothing at all," but rather because it is falsely understood to be something of great virtue.

Reclaiming Ourselves: Choosing to Become a Self Before God

For Kierkegaard, human sin was not so much a result of inflated and self-possessing egocentrism, but rather a consequence of a person's refusal to become a self, that is, self-abdication. He viewed despair over becoming a self as the common human condition, and he emphasized the importance of the self *choosing and becoming a self,* contending that "the self has the task of becoming itself in freedom" and choosing itself before God.

True, the nineteenth-century Dane also wrote against the self-aggrandizement that leads to pride, but he understood this to be only one manifestation of sin and the fall from God. For Kierkegaard, there were three manifestations of sin, all issuing from human despair over becoming a self: (1) "spiritlessness," the failure to realize one's possibility; (2) "weakness," the move to escape from one's self; and (3) "defiance," the attempt to affirm and master oneself by denying dependence on God. The "spiritless" one submits to nature; the "weak" one remains within the social conventions and necessities of life; the "defiant" one flouts nature and necessity and seeks to transcend the world as given. Spiritless and weak persons deny their possibility; they accept their lot and frequently give over their lives to the rule of others. Defiant persons ignore their finitude, seeking always to transcend limits and control others.

The Benedictine disciplines are most appropriate for those in Kierkegaard's third category, those who defiantly assert themselves without limit and concern for others. Defiant persons ignore finitude, refuse limitations, and seek to master life. Such expansive selves seek and accomplish great things, but eventually they flounder in possibility until exhausted. These need the discipline of humility to come rightly before God. But comparing Benedict's ladder with Kierkegaard's other two manifestations of sin as "spiritlessness" and "weakness" exposes how Benedict's formulations can actually contribute to these states. The spiritless and weak persons are so named because they *endure* their external reality; they do not imagine possibilities and nurture their own creativity. They are far too *content* to remain as they are and to *obey* the conventions of the day. Kierkegaard eloquently exposed the risk-avoiding, sedated existence of weakness: "Not to venture is prudent. And yet, precisely by not venturing it is so terribly easy to lose what would be hard to lose, however much one lost by risking, and in any case never this way, so easily, so completely, as if it were nothing at all—namely, oneself."[11]

What is of value here is Kierkegaard's perceptive recognition that self-abnegation as well as self-aggrandizement is despair leading to sin. Giving up oneself is no more faithful to God than seeking to master oneself. "Sin is: before God in despair not to will to be oneself, or before God in despair to will to be oneself."[12] For Kierkegaard, *the self must be grounded in God alone;* the self must not be lost in the crowd or given up to "matter-of-course" conventionality that results in the spirit being "secured against becoming aware."[13] Becoming aware, living an examined life, and questioning cultural assumptions were necessary fruits of knowing oneself to be grounded in God.

I am not seeking to exonerate women from sin, but I do want to *make the theological weight of self-abnegation more visible to women.* While we must be careful not to blame the victim, we must also be careful not to reinforce the victim by calling what is harmful a virtue. Giving up oneself—sometimes even in service to another—can be an act of sin if it is passive, splits the community into those who care and those who assert, and fails to hold other people accountable for their actions. In fact, this is increasingly recognized in the addiction literature where both addiction and co-dependence—inadvertent nurturing of the addiction through caregiving—are being analyzed. The *reality* of sin is not in dispute. It exists, it is pervasive, and all—men and women—are guilty of it. The *nature* of sin is varied, however. For some it takes the form of self-loss. Unfortunately, humility-oriented spiritual disciplines reinforce rather than mitigate this form of sin.

Conclusion

Several weeks ago I gave a children's message and preached a sermon on Judges 4, the story of Deborah. Recall that Deborah arose as judge in Israel, and she was distinguished by her abilities as a prophet and leader. She was proud, bold, and assertive. As I talked about this leader extraordinaire, I looked at the wide-eyed little girls and at the attentive teenage girls scattered throughout the pews. They were all engrossed in Deborah's story. I then thought back to another presentation I had given on Deborah a few years ago for a university women's study. During the study, one woman asked incredulously, "How come no one ever told me before about Deborah? I can't believe this is in the Bible!" That night I vowed that no girl with whom I came into contact would grow up without knowing about Deborah.

Joanne probably doesn't know about Deborah either, otherwise she would have valued the qualities that made this woman a leader. But Deborah *is* in the Bible, and the qualities that made her a remarkable leader are important Christian qualities. An empowering tradition is there for us to pass on to our daughters. My fantasy is that someday I'll sit in a fast-food restaurant when those wide-eyed little girls are teenagers, talking animatedly about their dreams and visions for the future. I'll intrude on their conversation and ask them where they got the confidence to assert themselves so boldly. They will tell me that it is from their religion, Presbyterianism. "We believe in boldness," they will announce.

When a gracious and renewing God is perceived to be at the center of our identity, which is the heart of Christian spirituality, then the boldness to assert ourselves is not a sin but a responsibility. The greatest hazard of all, losing the self, does not need to happen. We have noticed.

Notes

The quote from Søren Kierkegaard, appearing at the beginning of this chapter, is taken from a translation by Howard V. Hong and Edna H. Hong (Princeton, New Jersey: Princeton University Press, 1980), 32.

1. For a more extensive treatment of many of the issues raised here, see my book *Caretakers of Our Common House: Women's Development in Communities of Faith* (Nashville: Abingdon Press, 1997), chaps. 1, 4, 6.
2. *Wall Street Journal,* December 5, 1994, B1.
3. Robert Fulghum, *All I Really Need to Know I Learned in Kindergarten* (New York: Random House, 1988).
4. These awards bear a striking resemblance to the 1974 Sex Role Inventory, which uncovered preferred personality traits for men and women. Desirable traits for men included the following: leadership, aggressive, ambitious, analytical, assertive, competitive, decisive, strong personality, willingness to take risks. Desirable traits for women: affectionate, cheerful, compassionate, gentle, loves children, sensitive to the needs of others, sympathetic, yielding.
5. For example, see Carol Gilligan and Lyn Mikel Brown, *Meeting at the Crossroads: Women's Psychology and Girls' Development* (Cambridge: Harvard University Press, 1993).
6. Lesson for November 3, 1996, *Bible Discovery: Fall 1996* (Louisville: Presbyterian Publishing Company, 1996). Writers for Leader's Guide: Betty Eichler, Mickey Phillips, and Alex MacDonald. Writer for *Youth Pathways:* Mickey Phillips.
7. For a helpful commentary on Numbers, including this passage, see Katharine Doob Sakenfeld in *The Women's Bible Commentary,* ed. Carol A. Newsom and Sharon H. Ringe (Louisville: Westminster/John Knox Press, 1992), 45–51.
8. See Richard J. Foster and James Bryan Smith, eds., *Devotional Classics* (San Francisco: HarperCollins, 1993), 178–83.
9. See, for example, Clement of Alexandria, in *Christ the Educator,* trans. Simon P. Wood (New York: Fathers of the Church, 1954).
10. John Calvin, *Institutes of the Christian Religion,* 2 vols., ed. J. T. McNeill; trans. F. L. Battles (Philadelphia: Westminster Press, 1960), 3.2.1.
11. Søren Kierkegaard, *The Sickness Unto Death,* 13, 34, 35. Kierkegaard considered weakness the "feminine" form of despair and defiance its "masculine" form. Unfortunately, these are stereotypic categories that reduce the complexity of male and female experience.
12. Ibid., 81.
13. Ibid., 44.